Peace in a
Restless World

THE Mananam SERIES

(Mananam–Sanskrit for "Reflection upon the Truth")

Mananam: Reflection Upon Truth
Devotion
Emotions
Service: An Act of Worship
Vision of the Bhagavad Gītā
The Journey Called Life
The Light of Wisdom
Reincarnatiom: The Karmic Cycle
Māyā: The Divine Power
Embracing Love
At Home in the Universe
Beyond Ego
Happiness Through Integration
Living in Simplicity
Timeless Values
The Path of Love
Mind: Our Greatest Gift
The Sages Speak About Immortality
The Sages Speak About Life & Death
Divine Songs: The Gītās of India
Religion and Spirituality
Time and Beyond
Satsang with Swami Chinmayananda
About Sadhana
Divine Grace
Spirituality in Family Life
The Divine Mother
Beyond Stress
The Power of Faith
Joy: Our True Nature
Contemplation in a World of Action
Love and Forgiveness
(continued on inside back page)

THE mananam SERIES

Peace in a Restless World

CHINMAYA PUBLICATIONS
CHINMAYA MISSION WEST PUBLICATIONS DIVISION

Chinmaya Publications
Chinmaya Mission West Publications Division

P.O. Box 129
Piercy, CA 95587, USA

Distribution Office
560 Bridgetowne Pike
Langhorne, PA 19053
Phone: (215) 396-0390   Fax: (215) 396-9710
Toll Free: 1-888-CMW-READ (1-888-269-7323)
Internet: www.mananam.org
www.chinmayapublications.org

Central Chinmaya Mission Trust
Sandeepany Sadhanalaya
Saki Vihar Road
Mumbai, India 400 072

Copyright 2004 by Chinmaya Mission West.
All rights reserved. Published 2004.
Permission to reprint may be granted on request to:
Editor, editor@mananam.org
Printed in the United States of America.

Credits:
Editorial Advisor: *Swami Shantananda*
Series Editors: *Margaret Leuverink, Rashmi Mehrotra*
Associate Editor: *Neena Dev*
Cover Design: *Christine Wong, Neena Dev*
Inside Photographs: *David Dukes*
Production Manager: *Arun Mehrotra*

Library of Congress Catalog Card Number: 2004105580
ISBN 1-880687-56-9

Previously published and copyrighted materials are reprinted with the kind permission of the authors, publishers or copyright owners as listed below:

Abram, Irwin. *The Words of Peace, The Nobel Peace Prize Laureates of the Twentieth Century-Selections from their Acceptance Speeches.* © 2000 by the Nobel Foundation. Reprinted by permission of The Nobel Foundation, P.O. Box 5232, SE - 102 45 Stockholm, Sweden.

Roche, Douglas. *The Human Right to Peace.* © 2003 Novalis, Saint Paul University, 223 Main Street, Ottawa, Ontario K1S 1C4, Canada. www.novalis.ca.

Dear, John S. J. *Living Peace.* © 2001 by John Dear. Reprinted by permission of Doubleday, a division of Random House.

Easwaran, Eknath. *Original Goodness.* Founder of Blue Mountain Center for Meditation. © 1989. Reprinted by permission of Nilgiri Press, P. O. Box 256, Tomales, CA 94971. www.nilgiri.org.

H.H. Jagadguru Shankaracharya Shri Bharati Tirtha Mahaswamigal. *Jadadguru Calls for Inner Transformation. Tattvāloka*, Vol.4, 2000, p 4-6. Reprinted by permission of *Tattvāloka*, Abhinav Center No. 4 (Old19), Cooperative Colony, Chennai 600 018, India.

Hallengren, Anders. *Nelson Mandela and the Rainbow of Culture.* © 2004 The Nobel Foundation. Reprinted by permission of The Nobel Foundation, P.O. Box 5232, SE - 102 45 Stockholm, Sweden.

Maguire, Mairead Corrigan. *Peace is the Way*: Writings on Nonviolence from the Fellowship of Reconciliation edited by Walter Wink. Originally published in the June 1998 issue of *Fellowship* magazine and in *The Vision of Peace: Faith and Hope in Northern Ireland.* © 1999. Reprinted by permission of Fellowship of Reconciliation, Orbis Books, P.O. Box 308, Maryknoll, NY 10545-0308.

Rinpoche, Sogyal. *The Tibetan Book of Living and Dying*, edited by Patrick Gaffney & Andrew Harvey. © 1993 Rigpa Fellowship. Reprinted by permission of Harper Collins Publishers, Inc. M

Roof, Jonathan. *Pathways to God: A Study Guide to the Teachings of Sathya Sai Baba.* Printed in 1991. Reprinted by permission of Leela Press Inc., Rt 1, Box 339C, Faber, VA 22938.

Rush, Ann and John. "Peace Pilgrim" as reprinted in *Peace is the Way: Writings on Nonviolence from the Fellowship of Reconciliation* edited by Walter Wink. Originally published in the March 1982 issue of *Fellowship* magazine. Reprinted by permission of Orbis Books.

Swami Satprakshananda. *Vedanta Kesari* September 1992, Vol. 79. Reprinted by permission of *The Vedanta Kesari*, Sri Ramakrishna Math, 31 Ramakrishna Math Road, Mylapore, Chennai 600 004, India.

Vaswani, J.P. *East & West Series*, Volume 45, No. 10, October 2003. Reprinted by permission of *East and West Series*, 10 Sadhu Vaswani Path, Pune 411 001, India

Virajaprana, Pravrajika. *Vedanta Kesari* December 2003. Reprinted by permission of *The Vedanta Kesari,* Sri Ramakrishna Math, 31 Ramakrishna Math Road, Mylapore, Chennai 600 004.

Yogananda, Paramahansa. *Divine Romance.* © 1986 Self-Realization Fellowship. Reprinted by permission of Self-Realization Fellowship, 3880 San Rafael Avenue, Los Angeles, CA 90065.

Contents

Preface   ix

PART ONE
PEACE

I.	Peace in a Restless World	4
	by Swami Tejomayananda	
	The World	4
	Restlessness	5
	Peace	6
	Peace in the Phenomenal World	7
	Peace in the Social World	8
	Peace in the Individual	11
II.	The Significance of *Śānti*	17
	by Swami Pranavtīrtha	
III.	A Call for Transformation	19
	by Jagadguru Shankaracharya	
	Restoring Spirituality	20
	Problems Within	21
IV.	An Inquiry into Peace	22
	by Swami Chinmayananda	
	The Rippling Action of Desire	23
V.	A World without Boundaries	27
	by Paramahansa Yogananda	
	Free from Prejudices	28
	Expanding our Love	29
	International Understanding	30
	Learning to See God in All	31
	Clearing our Understanding	33
	Yoga Meditation	34
	Peace Will Reign	35

PART TWO
PEACEFUL LIVING

VI.	A Prescription for Peace	40
	by Pravrajika Virajaprana	
	Feel for Others	42
	Make the World Your Own	44
VII.	Building a Culture of Peace	47
	by Douglas Roche	
	Fifty Ways to Build World Peace	49
	Understand	51
	Participate	52
	Communicate	53
	Not Seeing the Blossom	54
VIII.	Peacemaking	56
	by Eknath Easwaran	
	Changing Our Way of Seeing	60
	Taking Responsibility	61
	Making Peace a Reality	64
IX.	Peace: Oneness with God	70
	by Jonathan Roof	
	(From the Teachings of Sathya Sai Baba)	
	Our Real Nature	71
	Inner Peace: Outer Peace	72
	How to Cultivate Peace	74

PART THREE
INNER PEACE

X.	Peace of Mind	80
	by Swami Tejomayananda	
	Peace is Always Present	81
	The Nature of Desire	84
	My-ness Causes Sorrow	85
	Separateness and Fear	86
	Gaining Peace	87

XI.	Peace of Mind: A Birthright *by J.P. Vaswani*	89
	Accept His Will	90
XII.	Making Peace with Yourself *by John Dear*	92
	The Daily Challenge	93
	Cultivating Inner Peace	95
	God's PeaceWithin Us	96
XIII.	Peacefully Remaining *by Sogyal Rinpoche*	99
	Natural Great Peace	100

PART FOUR
PEACEMAKERS

XIV.	The Words of Peace *Edited by Irwin Abrams* [Selections from Nobel Peace Prize Laureates]	108
XV.	Nelson Mandela and the Rainbow Culture *by Anders Hallengren*	116
	Equality and Pluralism	116
	The Development of "Color-blindedness"	117
	The Legacy of Mahatma Gandhi and Pandit Nehru	118
XVI.	Peace Pilgrim *by Ann and John Rush*	121
	Practicing the Simple Life	122
XVII.	Gandhi and the Ancient Wisdom of Nonviolence *by Mairead Corrigan Maguire*	125
	Creating a Culture of Nonviolence	127
XVIII.	Peace Prayers *Compiled by Editors*	131
	Gandhi Peace Prayers	131
	More Peace Prayers	133
	About the Authors	*136*
	Sanskrit Pronunciation Guide	*142*

Preface

Peace! We all want a peaceful mind, peaceful relationships, and a peaceful world. For when we are at peace we feel happy and content. Yet judging by the restlessness that we feel within ourselves and see all around us, it often appears that peace is far beyond our reach. But we need not lose hope, for in reality that elusive peace is closer than we realize. In fact peace is our own true nature. All our struggles in life are only to get back to our natural state of peacefulness. The authors in this book help us rediscover this eternal source of peace and happiness within.

In Part One, the authors explain the causes of restlessness in the phenomenal world (nature), in the society, and in the inner world of the mind. They encourage us to ask ourselves if we are doing everything we can to bring peace to these three worlds. In Part Two, the authors identify the practical steps we can take to help bring about harmony in our immediate surroundings. They show that through righteous (*dhārmika*) living, and opening our hearts in love we are able to uncover the peace that lies within us. In Part Three the authors illustrate how a life of peace begins in our own minds. From a peaceful mind, happiness radiates and all our interactions become positive and dynamic. When we enter into our inner depth we realize a basic truth, that oneness and peace are our inherent nature and that outward differences are only apparent. When the idea of separateness disappears we feel an inward expansion and an all-embracing love. This becomes the theme of Part Four, which shows examples of people who worked and lived for peace. Their exemplary lives show that it is possible to hold steadfast to inner peace while acting dynamically in the world.

A life of peace is possible! In fact, we all have a responsibility to bring about greater peacefulness, first in ourselves, then through peaceful interaction with everyone around us. When individual peace is attained, peacefulness expands to envelop the entire universe.

The Editors

PART ONE

Peace

If there is righteousness in the heart, there will be beauty in the character.

If there is beauty in the character, there will be harmony in the home.

When there is harmony in the home, there will be order in the nation.

When there is order in the nation, there will be peace in the world.

Author Unknown

Man must become established in the consciousness of his own true Self. The more he does so, the more peace will come in the world, the more he will find he has solved the problems of his life and the problems of his fellowmen — if that is what he wants. But if you don't have that consciousness you will make a mess of everything. The world will be like millions of madmen let loose from a lunatic asylum. … What can be more satisfying than to know that everything is transcendental Spirit and to know that Spirit is the all?

It is the reality, it is the truth; it is all the values. All the things that we seek exist in infinite measure in the Spirit. There is no other purpose to life. Know everything to be God, and everything will be fulfilled. For out of that knowledge come infinite love, infinite peace, infinite joy, infinite kindness and compassion, and infinite service. And if you have all these, what more do you want?

Swami Ashokananda

I

Peace in a Restless World

by Swami Tejomayananda

Every one of us is interested in knowing more about peace because everyone is seeking peace in life. But let me begin by saying that I do not have any magic solution. No one can give us peace; it is something that has to be discovered in our own hearts. Yet there are various aspects of this topic that I would like to share with you now, based on my understanding.

There are three main words in this topic: the world, restlessness, and peace. We have to understand each word clearly before we can proceed.

The World

When we speak of this world, there are three aspects to consider. One is the phenomenal world, which is made up of the forces of nature like the sun, moon, stars, planets, forests, and the living creatures. Also included are the five elements of nature: the earth, fire, water, space and air that are all around us. These are the forces of nature that are active and incessantly functioning with its unique laws.

The second is the social world with its distinctive dynamics of family, community, nations, economics, politics, science, technology, arts, music, and dance.

The third is the world of the individual. And although all communities and nations are governed by the same laws of the phenomenal world, we will find that every society, every nation, has its own distinct and unique character. This is obvious when we travel around the world. Societies have their own characteristics and an individual has his or her own psychology. Societies are made up of families and families are made up of many individuals, each one living in his or her own world, with different understanding and interpretations

After considering the three main aspects of the world — the phenomenal, the social, and the individual world — let us now try and understand the peace and restlessness of this world.

Restlessness

How is the phenomenal world restless? Do space, air, fire, water, and earth give us trouble? Is restlessness in them? It is true that sometimes nature seems to be restless — a huge fire may break out, or there may be flooding. That restlessness in the outer world causes restlessness in us, but as far as fire, water, air, sun, moon, stars, and planets are concerned, they just function, they follow the laws of nature. We cannot blame them. We do not hate water or stop using it because of floods. Even if fire burns down a building we don't hate fire. We may blame ourselves for being negligent in causing a fire, but even if the fire burns down our house, we continue to use it. It is the same with air, water, and everything else in this phenomenal world.

Let us now look at the social world. In society things happen that disturb us, either at the family level, the community level, or the national level. The law and order situation is deteriorating and people feel insecure. We find the economic situation volatile and that creates anxiety in us. The technology industry was making huge strides in California and other places, many large and small companies started up. But share markets and accounts were manipulated and many went bankrupt. Wars, civil unrest, riots, and terrorist attacks are also creating turmoil in our societies. So socially speaking there are many problems.

I have made an observation while traveling around the world that if we take a daily newspaper from each country and read the world news column, we will be surprised to see that names and places may differ but the news is the same. Disharmony, murder, kidnapping, looting, plundering, cheating, and scandals, are all breakdowns of the social order. And people everywhere complain that there is degradation in moral and ethical values and wonder what will happen to this world!

But human nature has a strange side. In real life we want to punish violence and crime, yet strangely enough, we want to read a thriller and watch a suspenseful movie. We like to watch and read about violence, but when it actually happens, we become angry and wonder what is happening to the society. We do not realize that the social restlessness that we see all around us is made up of individual restlessness. This defective human nature manifests itself in the chaos that we see all around us. What we see in human behavior is the resultant totality of what is in the hearts of all of us.

The restlessness in individual minds can arise for many reasons — physical pain, financial problems, emotional or relationship problems, and perhaps even spiritual problems.

We have seen three different worlds, the phenomenal, the social, and the individual. The nature of restlessness in each of these three worlds is unique. The phenomenal world is prone to the forces of nature, the social world suffers from disharmony and breakdown of social order, and the individual world suffers from a fragile peace shattered by never-ending desires.

Peace

When we say we want peace, what do we mean by peace? Just as restlessness can be of different kinds, so peace, too, can be of different kinds. If we go to a cremation or burial ground, there is peace, a dead peace. Do we want that kind of peace? When a person goes to sleep, then also he experiences peace, but it is a temporary peace. A mind filled with desires is restless, but when a desire is fulfilled, for a brief moment the mind is content and we feel peaceful. But for how long? By the time we say we are happy, already there is restlessness because we want something more, something different, or something new.

Some people think that peace is a passive, dull state, just doing nothing. Sometimes we take a tranquilizer and think that our mind has become tranquil, but we have simply dulled the mind so that the brain is not receiving any sensation at all. So what kind of peace do we want? If we understand peace as a lack of motivation, then we may wonder why peace is a goal of life at all. But we cannot accept a state of mind where there is no peace. So why do we want peace? The simple reason is that where peace is, happiness is! And we are all in search of happiness. Without peace, we cannot have any kind of happiness. Does anyone ever say, "I am very restless but I am happy?" Where is happiness for a restless, agitated person?

Only when there is peace — in the individual mind, in the society, or in the world of nature — then alone is there prosperity. Peace is needed for happiness, for prosperity, and for creativity. The peaceful mind becomes creative. This is when research work is possible. Great revelations of truth occurred to sages only in peace. When we are unable to solve a problem, because the mind is disturbed, the best thing is to sleep on it. Many times we will find that when the mind has rested, suddenly the solution is there. Frequently we consult another person to help us resolve our problems. He or she can give us great advice because that person's mind is at peace and is not emotionally involved. When the mind is clear, it is peaceful and intelligence shines forth.

Hence we have the need for peace at all levels — phenomenal, social, and individual.

Peace in the Phenomenal World

The question is what can we do to bring peace to the phenomenal world, which is governed by the forces of nature? The

Vedic mantras have the power to invoke peace from all the directions within the forces of nature. But we should remember that to a large extent we are responsible for the destructive effects occurring in nature. By cutting down trees and destroying forests we bring about great ecological imbalance. Every day we hear of global warming. We destroy nature with so much exploitation, and pollution all in the name of industrialization, warfare, defense, and progress. Vedic Scriptures teach us that if we are compelled to cut down one tree for any reason, we must plant ten trees elsewhere. Without planting new trees, we have no right to destroy forests. But these days there are concrete jungles everywhere, and the weather is changing rapidly. Then we blame God, and say that nature has failed us.

Vedic Scriptures say that one should worship the earth, the oceans, the wind, and the trees. But the ignorant consider it as superstitious worshiping. But now Earth Day is celebrated! The ancient wisdom is coming to life today in a different way. The Vedic concept of worship got distorted with time! Worshiping often meant the ritualistic offering. But the greatest worship of the ocean or water is not to pollute it! If we want nature to cooperate with us, to bless us, then it is necessary to learn to live in harmony with nature. Our attitude that we can conquer nature is full of arrogance and only brings disaster. Can we really stand up to the forces of nature? It is only God's grace, that in spite of our foolishness, nature still cooperates with us. By bringing about a caring attitude toward nature, peace is possible in the phenomenal world.

Peace in the Social World

What is the meaning of peace in the social world? Society is dynamic. There cannot be peace all the time. There will be disturbances. But if we want to bring about communal prosperity and harmony and a reasonable degree of peace, then that is possible, it is in our hands. There have been golden ages in the history of the world where peace and harmony reigned.

In the *Mahābhārata*, there is a beautiful dialogue between Yudhishthira [Pandava Prince] and his mother Kunti. Yudhishthira asked Mother Kunti: Is man the victim of circumstances or their master? Does the individual create his times or do the times create the individual? Mother Kunti replies to Yudhishthira with a very powerful *śloka* (*Mahābhārata,* 5:130.15): "Let there be no doubt in your mind — it is the king who creates his times. He creates the opportunity and he creates the situation. If there is change to be brought about in the society, the king is the master of circumstances."

In the *Bhagavad Gītā* (3:21), Lord Krishna clearly says: Whatever a great person or a great leader does, other people follow. All follow a standard that is set by a great person. So if peace, law and order, and prosperity are to be brought about, it becomes the duty of the ruling class, and the leaders to be role models. They cannot shrink from that responsibility.

In *Śrīmad Bhāgavatam* we find a story of a very great king, Raja Prithu. In a famous episode, the king addresses his citizens pointing out the three main duties of a king: Firstly, that he should be a protector. His duty is to bring law and order and a sense of security. That is the topmost priority. Without security there cannot be prosperity.

Secondly, he must be able to provide employment to all citizens. Unemployment brings all kinds of problems.

Thirdly and most importantly, it is a king's duty to provide education based on righteousness to all. Nowadays we call that value-based education. But there is no value base, just base values! When we look at educational institutions, and see the students' aspirations, we wonder what is going to happen to this world! Students eagerly wait to reach the legal drinking age so that they can party, some even carry guns, and drugs are rampant. When education is not rooted in righteousness, it is not education! Power is a great thing but if that power is uncontrolled and without direction that will create problems. The role of *dharma* (integrated living) is to give direction with discipline.

Raja Prithu continues to say that if a king fails to give his people the education needed to understand righteous living and fails to tell them what their duties and responsibilities are, and if they then commit crimes, all the sins will be accrued to the king and the king will have to suffer. That's how great the responsibilities were of the king, the ruling class, and the social leaders. And it is not always necessary that these leaders be wielders of political power. Many changes have been brought to society, not by politicians, but by great sages through their life examples.

Some may say that these are duties of a great man, but I am not great, it is not my responsibility! But that is an excuse, we cannot escape so easily. Every person is great to someone. I may look up to someone and someone may look up to me. In a family, the parents are everything for a child who regards them highly. Whether or not the child changes his opinion later in life, the parents have a great responsibility to influence their child's life with righteousness and greatness. Therefore each one of us has a great responsibility.

If a child is well behaved, people immediately want to know who the parents are. They must have given him great *saṁskāra* (inherent tendencies)! If a disciple does well, people want to know who is his or her guru. It is said that a tree is known by its fruit. So in a society, it is the responsibility of the social and political leaders, the government, and the spiritual leaders to bring about stability. History is full of examples when people felt helpless because those who were supposed to be their protectors had become their oppressors. At such times there were great devotees who kept their faith and devotion for God. Despite political disturbances, they sustained the society and did not allow it to disintegrate.

Our observation reveals underlying layers while interacting with individuals, organizations, and nations. At first, everything appears so beautiful and wonderful. But after a few days another layer begins to show. We begin to realize that there are undercurrents of strained relations, politics or subtle power-games. Despite all of this there is something that continues to hold the family, organization, community and the nation together. That integrating factor or force is called *dharma*. *Dharma* means that which integrates.

In the world today where there is so much terrorism, turbulence, and restlessness, we are still generally interacting with good people on a daily basis. Still there are more good people than bad. There is goodness because goodness alone is the sustaining factor. I will give you proof. Nowadays people are very fond of eating out. People like to go to Mexican, Italian, Chinese, Thai, and Indian restaurants. Now tell me, do you go into the kitchen to see who is cooking and how they are cooking? Are you afraid of being poisoned? No, we just go and eat at those restaurants. Hairdressers and barbers have knives and scissors in their hands but we willingly sit in their chairs and we're not afraid. When traveling by plane or train, we also have to have trust. Share markets are based on trust. Voting is based on trust. When we have surgery under general anesthesia, we don't know what will be done but we trust the surgeon. The entire world is sustained on trust. Invisible and unseen, that force is there. The great sages and saints strengthen it. Great leaders imbibe it and become role models in the society. If they do not, then there is fear of disintegration of the value system down to the level of the masses.

So we see that it is possible to bring about greater *śānti* (peace) at the social level. Political leaders have greater power because they can influence so many simply by enacting one law. But we also need great social leaders and great leaders in the fields of education and spirituality.

Peace in the Individual

Peace at the individual level is within the reach of every one of us. It is easy to make excuses for the restlessness in society or the phenomenal world, but when it comes to ourselves, there are no excuses. Here we have to find peace. Many people have found great peace in the midst of this restless world, which proves that only we are restless and we are superimposing that restlessness onto the world.

Let us think about this a little deeper and examine the causes of our individual restlessness. There are three basic aspects of our lives that cause us anxiety — our body, our actions, and our emotions (mind).

When our body suffers from pain and disease or from fear of disease, that in itself creates a lot of anxiety. So, we should first learn to take care of our physical health. Through proper exercise and right food, we can live a healthy life and we will enjoy great peace. When we are unhealthy, there is no enthusiasm, no energy, and every little problem becomes huge. Problems may never go away but a healthy body will give us the energy to deal with them as they come.

The second cause of restlessness in an individual is our action. In society, we are given a set of obligatory duties to be fulfilled and prohibited actions to be avoided. If we do not fulfill our duties, we become worried. And when we do a prohibited action, our mind becomes even more restless for fear of being caught. We should be very clear about this. If we want to have a really peaceful life at the level of actions, only obligatory duties, *kartavya karma*, should be done and we should avoid what is wrongful and prohibited. If we do not learn to discriminate between the do's and the don'ts then there will be problems. When that is done, our mind is at peace.

Let us now consider restlessness at the level of emotions. Our mind is a continuous flow of a variety of thoughts. Some thoughts create a very peaceful state of mind, some thoughts and emotions create only restlessness in the mind, and yet other thoughts create only dullness in the mind. There is a beautiful book on Vedanta called *Pañcadaśī* written by Swami Vidyananda, giving a wonderful analysis of these thought patterns. He says that our mind goes through different states, and different kinds of thoughts create different states in the mind. One is called "dull thought," *tāmasika*, causing ignorance, delusion, and sleepiness. All these thoughts only dull our mind. Thoughts that cause agitation in our mind are *rājasika* thoughts of passion, lust, anger, jealousy, or hatred, *sāttvika* thoughts are characterized by dispassion, faith, trust, devotion, love, and kindness. *Sāttvika* thoughts make our mind peaceful, creative, energetic, and objective. In the *sāttvika* state there is conservation of energy, while in the others there is dissipation of energy.

Relationships are a very important aspect of our emotional state. Our mind becomes restless and a lot of tension is created when our relationships are strained. But when relationships are good, things are beautiful. If there is mutual love between people then laws, rules, and regulations are not needed. When there is love, each person wants to give and give — there is no need for rules. But if there is no love, not a single rule will work. When there is love, people talk *to* one another, but when there is no love, they talk *at* each other.

If relationships are based on material considerations, they will not last because the nature of matter is to change, decay, and perish. In material considerations we seek some satisfaction, whether appreciation, or recognition, or some tangible gain. Wise people have a spiritual relationship even with material things. They value this body, which is matter, as the most precious gift, which is meant for seeking the realization of Truth. This body is the primary means for fulfilling *dharma* and attaining liberation. They take care of the body with that attitude. When they have material wealth, they say it is meant for serving everyone, it is God's gift. Here the body or material wealth never causes bondage for them. But in our case, we perform good deeds, expecting some kind of material gain. And if material wealth does not come, we say, "What is the use of doing good things if I get nothing from it!"

Even our relationship with God is bound by our need to

have our troubles removed and desires fulfilled. If we want to have peace of mind, then like the wise sages, all our relationships starting with the physical body, with wealth, with people, with our actions, with our emotions, and with God, should be based on spiritual considerations.

An enlightened sage is totally at peace and experiences happiness, for he has determined and experienced the nature of Truth, which is the nature of Peace itself. That Peace is our True Self. In the *Māṇḍūkya Upaniṣad*, it is the Self, which is *śānti*, peace itself, which is non-dual. When that is realized there is supreme peace, *param śānti*.

At the emotional level, if our heart is filled with love for God, then there is peace. At the level of relationships, if our love and relationships are based on spiritual and not material considerations, then there is peace. At the level of action, when we are steadfast in the performance of our duty while avoiding prohibited actions, then there is peace. At the physical level, having good health provides peace.

The wise man lives in the material world but it does not bind him. He can have wealth, but if that wealth is used for serving others that wealth will not bind him. In the Upanishads, all the rishis pray for wealth, but before wealth they ask for right understanding and right attitude, then that wealth will be a great blessing. But if right understanding is not there, that wealth will become a curse. In *karma yoga* the work we do must be in fulfillment of our obligatory duties. Lord Krishna clearly says: "Dedicate all work to Me. Just as the lotus leaf lives in the water but remains untouched by it, similarly such men live in the world of karma, but karma does not bind them because it is dedicated to God." Thus in *Karma Yoga*, the performance of duty is the number one criteria. Dedication of our work to God as worship is the second criteria. And the third criteria is no attachment to the fruits of our actions. Whatever result comes, it is taken as *prasāda*, as a blessing.

Just think! If we dedicate our life to the Lord, the results

PEACE IN A RESTLESS WORLD

also belong to Him. Why should we become restless? We become restless and anxious because we want something for ourselves. Lord Krishna in the *Bhagavad Gītā* says that the moment you renounce attachment to the result of action there will be *śānti, śānti, śānti*.

There is a great relationship between the heart and the stomach. When the heart is full, the stomach automatically gets full. When a person is restless he eats too much junk food. But when a heart is filled with love of God, and realization of Truth, then he becomes like a vast, deep ocean, there is utter fullness. But the person who always wants something will always feel empty, because from the moment an object comes, already he wants something else.

Now, in this restless vast global world, is it possible to attain a dynamic peace? Yes, the solution is in our own hands. For we can all make an effort to become healthier, to remain steadfast in our duties, and have the right attitude of devotion. Why can't we fill our hearts with love? Why that feeling of emptiness? It is totally in our control. It does not depend upon the phenomenal world or the social world. No one can stop us from realizing Truth. If we are not getting up early, who is at fault? Who stops us from loving God and dedicating all actions to Him? No one! Therefore, we have no reason to complain.

Bhikṣu Gītā says, "The cause of my sorrow, agitation, or restlessness is none of these people, not the planets, it is only my own mind that has wrong emotions, and wrong attitudes." And then we say that the world is restless. Only we are troubled and restless. We will become dynamic people if we can find this peace of spiritual realization.

We began this talk from a material standpoint and have arrived at the spiritual. This analysis is given so beautifully and clearly in our scriptures. I have given you their magic words. Who can stop us from living them? Just do it and experience the peace, *śānti*.

Śānti is called *Satyam* (Truth). But in our life we are so caught up in our illusions that we experience *aśānti — asatyam* (falsehood). We create the disturbances and our mind projects the inner restlessness. The greatest service we can do in this world is to mind our own business and take care of our own mind. But we are poking our nose in everyone's affairs and want to improve everyone, but ourselves. A change is required in all of us. With this vision of fullness, Shri Gurudev, Swami Chinmayananda, started his magnificent work. Peace inside will only radiate outside. Your peaceful light will touch others and it will continue to spread like rippling waves. Only then is lasting peace possible.

II

The Significance of Śānti

by Swami Pranavtirtha

[The following article is translated by Anu Parmar from the teachings of Swami Pranavtirtha]

In Vedic tradition *Śānti* is chanted three times at the conclusion of every prayer session. This is not for the sake of "sealing a deal" as is done by the auctioneers. But, in fact, it is for the three types of peace that we seek and ask for from the Lord.

There are only three sources that shatter and disturb our peace and cause our restlessness. The first is from the gross, tangible world of matter; the second is from the intangible and less subtle world of energy; and the third is from the world of our inner and most subtle self.

All life and inanimate objects are made up of five elements — the *pañca mahābhūta* — earth, water, fire, air, and ether. The probability and possibility of chaos and restlessness caused by these elements is immense. Earthquakes, flood, famine, wars, are all examples of the chaos of the physical, material world. So the very first *śāntiḥ* we ask for is to be protected from the agitations caused by the world of matter — *ādhibhautika*, that which is made of the five *bhūta* (elements). We ask for peace from this physical world.

The second cause of restlessness and anxiety lies in the "unseen forces." The forces in the universe that are more subtle than the material world. These forces are the energy from the movement of the planets, the pull of our destiny — our relationships with friends, family, and neighbors — things that we cannot see but know to be. This is called *ādhidaivika* that which pertains to the *deva* — unseen energy. This second *śāntiḥ* we ask is for the peace from this metaphysical world.

The third source of our anxiety is caused solely by ourselves. It is subtle and closest to us. Our ignorance, mental anguish, ill health, injury, various diseases are all disturbances born of the body and the mind. This is called *ādhyātmika*, that which pertains to our inner self, our soul. We ask for peace from our inner being.

When we chant *śāntiḥ* three times, we begin the first with a loud voice, which signifies the grosser and farther world. The second *śāntiḥ* is chanted less loudly, which signifies the more subtle and closer world. The last *śāntiḥ* we say very quietly as if speaking to ourselves, which signifies the subtlest and closest world.

In this way, we ask with intelligence and understanding for peace from all these three dimensions. When we experience tranquility for a short while, we call it *śāntiḥ* — peace. But this is not true peace. In reality there are thousands of reasons for our unhappiness and anxiety and they are all encapsulated in the only three sources; *ādhibhautika* – the physical world, *ādhidaivika* – the metaphysical world and *ādhyātmika* – our inner world. The Vedic rishis perfected the art of asking so completely and beautifully! *Śāntiḥ, Śāntiḥ, Śāntiḥ*. Peace, Peace, Peace.

III

A Call for Transformation

by Jagadguru Shri Bharati Tirtha Mahaswamigal

[This message of H.H. Jagadguru Shankaracharya Shri Bharati Tirtha Mahaswamigal, was read by his Secretary at the Millenium World Summit Conference of religious and spiritual leaders held at the UN, New York, August 28-31, 2000]

At the outset I wish to thank the organizers of the summit for giving me this opportunity to address this august assembly. In many parts of the world we witness terrible wars, terrorists activity, and many other atrocities. It causes great anguish to see many people resorting to violence and causing injury to life.

It is a great sin to hurt others in any way. It does not matter if we cannot do good to others, but we should never hurt them. The greatest service one can do to humanity is not to hurt anyone by thought, word, or action, this is *ahiṁsā*, non-hurtfulness.

Greed is at the bottom of all the problems of the world, greed for wealth, greed for power, and worst of all, greed for name and fame. It is natural for us to want to lead a happy and comfortable life. However, we should set a limit to our wants.

Because of the greed of a few individuals, millions of innocent people have been massacred. Contentment is most essential for humanity. Without it, one cannot be happy even if one gets everything that is in the world. All of us should be content with what God has given. Only then can we live in peace and let others live in peace.

JAGADGURU BHARATI TIRTHA MAHASWAMIGAL

The task before us, religious leaders, is daunting. We have to educate the people of the need for spirituality and restore their faith in the scriptures and God. We have to teach them what is good [right] and what is bad [wrong].

Restoring Spirituality

Humanity has moved away from God and spirituality. Hence, so many violent and criminal activities are taking place. Spirituality is the need of the hour. By our concentrated efforts we must restore spirituality to its rightful place.

In many parts of the globe we find terrible conflicts taking place due to religious intolerance. All religions worship the same God. All religions have the same goal and that is God-realization. Just as you can reach the ocean by traveling on any river you can reach God by following any religion.

In God's creation nothing happens without a divine purpose. If only one religion was enough for all, God would not have created so many diverse religions. The very fact that so many diverse religions co-exist implies that all of them are necessary for humanity. Let us work together to infuse love and tolerance in the hearts of all and remove religious intolerance and hatred.

Poverty is another reason why theft, robbery, arson, murder, and other crimes occur. Poverty is a man-made problem. God has created plenty for everyone. Look at the animals, do you see any poor animals? Do you see any animal dying without food? Hardly ever. But we see billions of people living in inhuman conditions on streets and dirty slums. Why? Because a few people have hoarded the wealth that belongs to all. So the others suffer.

If each affluent person simply helps one poor person to stand on his feet, then we will be able to completely eradicate poverty very quickly. Little drops make the ocean. If all rich people help a bit, then poverty can be eliminated soon.

It is meaningless to live only for ourselves, if we live only for own happiness we would be worse than even animals. A tree does not eat its delicious fruits. It gives it to others. A cow does not drink its milk. It gives it to others. True happiness lies in helping and serving others.

The value of social service is recognized by all religions. All of us here are doing excellent work by running schools, hospitals, orphanages and old age homes for the poor and the needy. But much more remains to be done. Billions are materially poor and are crying for our help. Billions are spiritually poor and are in dire need of our assistance. We must remove both types of poverty. Only then can Mother Earth turn into a heaven of peace and happiness.

Problems Within

The violence, tension, and unrest that we behold in the world around us are actually not the real problems that plague us. The real problem lies within us. Our minds have become heavily polluted. Worldly desires and attachments damage our minds day and night. Due to ignorance we have lost the ability to distinguish between good and evil. We have lost touch with the God who dwells inside us. This inner turmoil is the root cause of all the evils of the world. Only through inner transformation of each and every human being can we transform earth into a veritable heaven on a permanent basis. All other measures can only give short-term results.

Spirituality alone can save our beautiful planet. There is absolutely no alternative to spirituality. The darkness of worldliness has enveloped Mother Earth. It is most appropriate that at this critical juncture, the UN hosted this historic Millennium World Peace Summit of religious and spiritual leaders.

Religion and spirituality alone can bring solace to this world. Very soon, the dark night of senseless materialism shall go away. The golden radiant sun of spirituality is about to rise and shower the rays of knowledge, love, peace, and happiness on our beloved earth.

IV

An Inquiry into Peace

by Swami Chinmayananda

Had man been just an animal, he would not need anything more than physical comforts and security, but as a highly evolved and developed psychological being, he wants emotional satisfaction. And being highly intellectual he is restless and impatient with all imperfections. He is not merely a physical structure consisting of his body; he has a mind and intellect also. The materialistic needs of the body can satisfy only the physical man, which is only a third of an individual; two thirds of the individual is not taken into consideration when materialism strives to satisfy merely the basic needs in a community.

Materialism is wonderful, no doubt, but it burdens man with an endless anxiety and craving to possess more and more, to acquire and aggrandize and to live with slavish attachment. It is natural for man to seek his fulfillment and happiness only in thoughtless intemperance, in toiling for and reaching the temporary gratification of his physical passions, mental urges, and intellectual hungers. Is it not a fact that, in recent times, more people are killed by worry than by work? Man in his present misconceived civilization has learned to waste himself and his precious time in the inevitable trifles and tensions that beset his life.

Acquiring and spending, we lay waste our powers. Each of us seeks the same goal. We all want nothing but unadulterated, unbroken, absolute joy and peace among the sensual objects that constitute our world. But sensual objects have a false glitter of joy about them. The joy soon fades away. At the loss of such joy, the worldly seekers strive hard to multiply their capacity for purchasing more and more of the same fleeting joys.

If peace and joy is the goal of every living being, and all our day-to-day struggles are to gain that peace, it is quite natural to ask, "What is peace?" Surely we realize that the question is not about any phenomenon in nature outside, where laboratory experiments and factual representations could facilitate understanding. The question is essentially a subjective inquiry into a state of satisfaction felt within and lived by the individual with or without reference to the external circumstances of the world outside. By peace, we mean a mental condition in the subject lived by him and recognized as such in the absolute sorrow-less silence in his own within. Therefore only by looking within, and observing the happenings and occurrences during the various mental conditions, can we conduct an inquiry into peace.

In short, self-analysis and introspection are the very beginnings of all philosophical inquiries into self-perfection. They are the perfect means of achieving a true vital blissful living. As long as the values respected in life are of indulgence in feeding the sensual demands, attention gets diverted outward, and the chaos within cannot be ended. We will therefore strive to understand the entire inner processes by which the experiencer can adjust and purify his equipment.

The Rippling Action of Desire

In every one of us there are, at any given moment, a hundred desires struggling to seek their fulfillment. In those rare lucky ones among us who gain in life at least a seeming fulfillment of some of their desires, we observe how each fulfillment is but the breeding ground for a dozen other complimentary desires — each an attempt to complete the imperfections of the phantom joy achieved!

Let us analyze a single desire and observe what exactly happens within us. "If only I had a son" is the beginning of an entire unending chain of life-long anxieties. The person wishing for a son feels that the available circumstances in his life do not serve his conception of full or complete joy, and do not therefore give him that texture of joy or peace which he demands of life. His solution slowly gets crystallized in his vague desire that a son would complete his joy. His desire is thus an unconscious effort on his part to have a fuller expression of himself.

The desire for a son is at the beginning only a localized disturbance in the mental lake. But a million ringlets of concentric disturbance follow, and the widening ripples of thought come to splash upon the vast banks. The desire motivates an endless array of thoughts; thoughts thus motivated by each desire get projected into the waking state world, and among its sense objects they manifest as actions. Successful actions end in their desired fruit — which is but the objectification of the subjective desire.

The individual, tortured by his own thought, cannot contain himself within. His own thoughts, as they gain vitality from his desire, soon make him their slave. When these thoughts find their expression, then the seeking of a bride, the meeting, the talk, the transaction, the procession, and the wedding happen. The desire for a son, which caused the inner whirlwind, dragging him through a distance of sweat and worry, at last condemns him to the thorny fields of fatherhood. "Ah! My son has arrived! My great son!"

All joy, but alas, only for a fleeting moment! The joy is immediately followed by his constant run for the milk-powder and feeding-bottle, the doctor, the nurse, and the chemist! Soon the individual is shuttled between the toyshops and the home, the school and theater, the bookshops, and so on. Every day that very thing-of-joy, the son, provides for the father a hundred hopes, fears, plans, failures, disappointments, and sorrows.

"But at least in that sacred moment when he cried out 'my son,' don't you think he had a taste of some joy?" If one is tempted to ask thus, one is perfectly right. Hence it is that in the very beginning, we admitted that sense objects do provide joy, but only a false glitter of joy.

"If there be any joy-content at all in the sense objects, why don't we arrest the moment of our experience and prolong it to any desired length of time?" Let us patiently continue our inquiry; probably we may come to discover the very secret of permanent joy.

We have observed how the desire for a son caused a storm of thoughts, how they manifested in the world outside as actions, and how the desire for a son had objectified, as it were, for the happy father. The father at the birth of his child feels extremely happy. Why? Let us find out exactly what happens within him the moment he knows that his desire for a son has been fulfilled; say, at the moment of the first cry of the child or at that inspiring moment when a foot-long tender thing placed between folds of cloth is laid in the father's lap. The inner ripples or agitation suddenly settle down.

The thought-disturbances caused on the shore of the desire sink down; for a split moment, the mental stuff in its liquid clearness reflects the glory within. "Ah! The joy!" But the next moment it is gone. Why? A thousand other desires regarding the son and his comforts, the mother and her health, the nurse and her conveniences, all come up to disturb the glory-reflecting medium, the stilled mind.

So then, the mind is at once the breeding ground of desires, the dung-heap of contending thoughts, and also the glorious castle of perfect joy! When the mind is stilled, it ceases erupting its scorching lava of thoughts, and peace is the subjective experience. Peace is joy. This is why, in peaceful dreamless sleep, every living creature feels nothing but joy.

From what we have so far observed, it can be inferred that the joy-in-the-son was not in the son, but in the particular condition within the mind that the birth of the son occasioned. So then, the source of joy is not in the external world of objects, but is deep within us. Whenever the mind is at perfect rest, an effulgent flood of the inner bliss pours out its satisfying joy.

The desire for objects creates disturbances that shatter our real nature of *śānti*, peace. The struggle and urgency of the individual to get his desire fulfilled represents the urge of truth to assert itself. The spirit within is asserting to come back to its essential state of fullness. The tension in the bowstring is from the consistent pull of the stem of the bow to regain its straight nature. The tension of life and its pains are from the benign pull of the Truth upon untruth!

We have thus understood that desire breeds thoughts and thoughts propel us to action. When the actions end in successful fruition, the result is the calming of the thought-storm, which in its turn produces the feeling of joy and peace in the subject. Hence the conclusion is self-evident; the solution for all the sorrows of life now becomes an open secret. Renounce desire — thoughts will end. When the desire agitations are hushed up, eternal peace is experienced. This experiencing of the all-full satisfaction and contentment, which is independent of the external world and the daily circumstances, is the perfect, achievable, and to-be-achieved goal of life.

V

A World without Boundaries

by *Paramahansa Yogananda*

[Opening talk at a banquet at the Self-Realization Fellowship Second Temple, Los Angeles, California, February 26, 1939.]

Wherever different minds meet in the spirit of fellowship, there we find a great harmony, peace, happiness, understanding, and cooperation in life's activities. With so many troubles plaguing this earth of ours — a miniature world war going on in Europe, nation tearing at nation — never before was there a greater necessity for peace than now.

    I believe there will always be wars, until perchance we all become so spiritual that by the evolution of our individual natures we will make war unnecessary. No matter what their differences, if great minds such as Jesus, Krishna, Buddha, Mohammed sat together, they would never use the engines of science to try to destroy each other. Where there is understanding, peace reigns. Why must people feel it necessary to fight? The power of guns evokes no wisdom, nor has it ever accomplished lasting peace.

    War is like poison in the system. When we have toxins in our body, that impurity has to get out somehow. So we suffer from disease. Likewise, when there is too much selfishness in the international system, that poison breaks out in the world as the disease of war. Many people are killed, and then for a little while there is a lull. But war comes again — and will come again and again — as long as there will be ignorance, and as long as the individual man has not become a perfect citizen of the world.

God gave us intelligence, and He placed us in an environment where we must use that intelligence. The universe is like a shell, and we are like little chicks moving about within it. But what is beyond this shell of matter? What is beyond its three dimensions? We must penetrate space and know the workings of that other world out of which this one has come. We should use our intelligence to analyze the mysteries of life and to explore the secrets the heavenly Father has hidden behind nature. How much better use of intelligence this would be, than the creation of bigger and more destructive instruments of war. We must use our intelligence to have peace among ourselves.

Free from Prejudices

Why not follow a process of education in which, rather than nurturing hatred toward nations that are different from our own, we try by love to create understanding? Understanding is extremely necessary. But just as some people are shortsighted and some are farsighted, so is our understanding. It is often clouded by many prejudices. Our vision is obscured from our very birth by the prejudices of family, race, and nation. Prejudice is a principal cause of war between brother nations. We shall never understand our own-selves or others, unless we keep our understanding free from all clouds of prejudice.

We so love our own thoughts that we can't always understand what the other person is thinking. We are cooped up in a little pen of our own concepts; just like the little frog that lived in a well: When a frog from a huge lake fell into the well and told him about his vast home, the little frog only laughed and wouldn't believe him. He had never seen anything beyond the confines of the well, and was thoroughly convinced that his home was the largest body of water there could possibly be. This is the limited attitude of nations as well as individuals.

A WORLD WITHOUT BOUNDARIES

Each nation thinks its views are best.

We have to learn to give unceasing understanding to all, even to those who misunderstand us. I give you an illustration: C can analyze D fairly well, so he thinks he can understand everybody else. But he knows nothing about B, who is sitting behind C and D, and thinks he understands both of them. And behind B is A, who sees B, C, and D, and therefore thinks he understands everyone. It is human nature to think we know better than anyone else. But the only way to truly know anything is by cultivating divine understanding.

Expanding Our Love

International understanding is much clouded by lack of realization that individual happiness is included in family happiness, family happiness in community happiness, community happiness in national happiness, and national happiness in international happiness.

Love of family is inherently strong. Through family love, God became the father to love you through wisdom, and He became the mother because He wanted to give you unconditional love. God became the lover and the beloved to unite souls in an expanded love. He became the friend to unite souls in a pure, impersonal love that makes no demands. In friendship there is no compulsion; it comes through the choice of the heart. Such friendship should exist between husband and wife, child and parent, in all human relations. Friendship is a great factor in bringing peace in the international family of the world.

No one can love his nation without learning the first lesson in love, which is to love his family. The baby's initial cries are for milk, but soon it invests its love in the mother and father. Then, as it grows older, it learns to love its country. When that soul becomes Christlike, it begins to love the world.

You are a member of the worldwide human race. Don't forget it. You must love the world as you love your nation and your family. This is difficult to learn, but the task of Self-Realization Fellowship is to show you how. We teach that it is by fellowship with God that fellowship with man must be established; because only when you know God and see Him in all can you love the Jew and Christian, Muslim and Hindu, with the same spirit. I was taught this as a child, but it was more or less a forced intellectual concept. It wasn't an understanding from within. I tried to love the whole world, but it was not easy. As soon as I looked at my family, my love lost itself there. But one by one, many of those dearest to me died. I thought that nature was very cruel. Then I began to realize that my love was undergoing discipline; that I was to expand my love, not limit it to my family. God showed me that it was He whom I loved in my loved ones. Then, from within, my love began to expand to all. I could no longer feel partiality toward family. When I returned to India in 1935, I saw that this was true. Except for the love Father gave me, I felt like a stranger when I visited the family home.

Therefore, through family life and then through national life, God is schooling every individual to understand his international family, that we may have a United States of the World with Truth as our guide.

International Understanding

We are all aliens here. No territory belongs permanently to any country. The hand of time eventually erases all nations. Their boundaries don't last, because they represent divisions that have been carved out by force. I believe a time will come when in greater understanding we shall have no boundaries anymore. We shall call the earth our country; and we shall, by process of justice and international assembly, distribute unselfishly the goods of the world according to the needs of the people. But equality cannot be established by force; it must come from the heart. The greatest blessing would be to develop international understanding by which we may realize this truth.

These ideals should be taught in all the schools. Just as it would be a sin to teach everyone to "love your family; it doesn't matter what happens to your country," so it is a sin to teach love of country that militates against your greater world family. When in every school love of country is over-emphasized, it sows the seeds of misunderstanding and even hatred toward other nations. How dare we spoil children by teaching them the kind of patriotism in which there are seeds of hatred! Unless you love your country, you cannot love the world; but children should be taught also to love other countries as they love their own. That is the principle of God.

Learning to See God in All

So you see, we must dissociate our wisdom from all environmental influences. If we can learn to understand others, and to free our minds from all prejudices born of environment, we begin to express the perfect image of God within us and to find it in all. "But as many as received him, to them gave he power to become the sons of God." (John 1:12) The light of the sun falls equally on the diamond and the charcoal; but the diamond, by its transparency, reflects the sun more. Lord Krishna taught that because the wisdom in man is covered by ignorance, and because man chooses to misuse his independence to nurture that ignorance, he doesn't reflect the true image of God that is within him. But in all those who use the power of the mind to be good the power of Spirit will manifest. If we can *receive* that power of Spirit then we become true sons of God. And we must learn to see the light of God falling on both His good and bad children. Peace will come when we discipline our hearts to see God in all, not just in those who love us or whom we think of as our own.

Peace is not something that you and I or a few great souls can create at once, by command. Even a million Christs or Krishnas could not do it. Try as he would, Lord Krishna could not prevent the great war between the Pandavas and Kauravas, which is described in the *Mahābbārata*. All humanity has to become Christ-like to bring peace on earth. When each one of us shapes his life according to the wisdom and example of a Christ, a Krishna, a Buddha, we can have peace here, not before. We must start now, with ourselves. We should try to be like the divine ones who have come on earth again and again to show us the way. By our loving each other and keeping our understanding clear, as they taught and exemplified, peace can come.

Each individual in a family and community should strive to live peacefully with others. Peace must begin in the home and in the schools. In the classrooms we must teach international patriotism — to love the world as Jesus, Krishna — as the great masters have taught, and not to do anything that would lead to international discomfort. It is not our nationality or our color that we should be proud of, but our understanding. We should cultivate our understanding and use it to determine what is truly best for family happiness, national happiness, and international happiness. International happiness should include the well-being of the nation, the community, and the family. The standard of legislation should be merit, not color of skin or any other class distinction. These are the ideals to be taught to children.

As long as God's children differentiate, "We are Hindus, you are Americans; we are Germans, you are English," so long will they be bound by delusion and the world divided. Much war and suffering and destruction will be prevented if we cease to emphasize differences and learn to love all without distinction or prejudice. Be more proud that you are made in the image of God than that you are of a certain nationality for "American" and "Indian" and all the other nationalities are just outer coats, which in time will be discarded. But you are a child of God throughout eternity. Isn't it better to teach that ideal to your children? It is the only way to peace: Establish the true ideals of peace in the schools, and live peace in your own life.

A WORLD WITHOUT BOUNDARIES

Clearing our Understanding

If we analyze individual psychology, we find that all human beings are passing through one of four states. When a desire is fulfilled we are happy. When a desire is contradicted we are unhappy. Between these two states is indifference; we are neither happy nor unhappy. Beyond these three states is peace. If we can clear our understanding of all selfish prejudices — individual, family, and national — we can reach that state of peace.

Just think, if Hitler and other dictators and world aggressors had had no personal or national selfishness, how many wars would have been averted. I would like to see one qualified person attain to the presidency just for the sake of the country. Lincoln was such a one. I cannot think of him without thinking of his aspirations for all mankind. But most politicians seek office for their own advantage, and the advantage of those communities and causes that are closest to them personally. The love of nation of a Lincoln or a Gandhi is based on wisdom. The ambitions of puny politicians do great harm against the permanency of this or any country.

So patriotism must not bring wars and troubles in its wake. What is the value of a patriotism that destroys life, that kills innocent men, women, and children? War is supposed to show the nation's love of country. But that is not the right way to show it. The way to demonstrate true patriotism is to behave as children of God, and to give divine understanding to all people. "All they that take the sword shall perish with the sword." (Matthew 26:52) Divine Love is greater than the power of the sword. Greater than all the swords in the world is understanding.

Today, the best country to live in is America. I am not saying this to flatter you but because it is the truth. Here you have freedoms and material advantages and opportunities unknown in many other nations. Don't abuse those privileges and blessings. Remember that the only justification for life is to unravel the mysteries of this universe. The only justification for human existence is to find God. The Lord hopes you will learn to love the Giver more than all His material gifts.

Yoga Meditation

Out of the cosmic tomes of truth, India developed the Yoga system, the science of oneness — oneness of the soul with God; oneness with the principles of eternal righteousness; with the universe; and with all mankind. The sage Patanjali formulated the *Yoga* system into eight steps for achieving the goal:
1. Avoid unrighteous behavior — *yama*.
2. Follow certain moral and spiritual precepts — *niyama*.
3. Learn to be still in body and mind, for where motion ceases, there begins the perception of God — *āsana*.
4. While concentrating on the state of peace, practice control of the life force in the body — *prāṇāyāma*.
5. When your mind is your own, that is, under your control through *prāṇāyāma* then you can give it to God — *pratyāhāra*.
6. Then begins meditation: first, concentrate on one of God's cosmic manifestations such as love, wisdom, and joy — *dharaṇā*.
7. What follows in meditation is an expansion of the realization of God's infinite omnipresent nature — *dhyāna*.
8. When the soul merges as one with God, who is ever existing, ever conscious, ever new Bliss, that is the goal — *samādhī*.

The joy of God can never be exhausted. He is sufficient, the purpose and the aim of existence. True understanding comes when we feel God as the great bliss of meditation. And peace is the first proof of His presence.

To have peace we must love more, but we cannot love people unconditionally unless we know God. The soul is absolutely perfect, but when identified with the body as ego, its expression becomes distorted by human imperfections. If human beings were only these imperfect bodies and minds, there would be some justification for prejudices and divisions. But we are all souls, made in God's image. So *Yoga* teaches us to know the divine nature in ourselves and others. Through *yoga* meditation we can know that we are gods.

Peace Will Reign

I believe that if every citizen in the world is taught to *commune* with God (not merely to know Him intellectually), then peace can reign; not before. When by persistence in meditation you realize God through communion with Him, your heart is prepared to embrace all humanity.

I am neither a Hindu nor an American. Humanity is my race, and no one on earth can make me feel otherwise. Prejudice and exclusiveness are so childish. We are here for just a little while and then whisked away. We must remember only that we are children of God. I love all countries as I love my India. And my prayer to you is that you love all nations as you love America. God created a diverse world to teach you to forget your physical differences with other races; and, from the debris of misunderstanding and prejudice, to salvage your understanding and use it to make an effort to know Him as our one Father.

Therefore, my friends resolve that you will love the world as your own nation, and that you will love your nation as you love your family. Through this understanding you will help to establish a world family on the indestructible foundation of wisdom. Follow the ways of God. Set a time apart each day to meditate on Him. When you commune with God, you shall feel toward everyone as toward your own. No one can ever make me feel He is not mine. All human beings are God's children, and He is my Father.

PART TWO

Peaceful Living

*He is happiest,
Be he a king or peasant,
Who finds his peace at home.*

Johann W. Goethe

People in the peace movement can write very good protest letters, but they are not so skilled at writing love letters. We need to learn to write letters to the Congress and the President that they will want to read, and not just throw away. The way we speak, the kind of understanding, the kind of language we use should not turn people off. The President is a person like any of us. Can the peace movement talk in loving speech, showing the way for peace? I think that will depend on whether the people in the peace movement can "be peace." Because without being peace, we cannot do anything for peace. If we cannot smile, we cannot help other people smile. If we are not peaceful, then we cannot contribute to the peace movement.

I hope we can offer a new dimension to the peace movement. The peace movement often is filled with anger and hatred and does not fulfill the role we expect of it. A fresh way of being peace or making peace is needed. That is why it is so important for us to practice mindfulness, to acquire the capacity to look, to see, and to understand. It would be wonderful if we could bring to the peace movement our non-dualistic way of looking at things. That alone would diminish hatred and aggression. Peace work means, first of all being peace. We rely on each other. Our children are relying on us in order for them to have a future. ...

Thich Nhat Hanh
Peace is Every Step

VI

A Prescription for Peace

by *Pravrajika Virajaprana*

> I tell you one thing:
> "If you want peace, do not find fault with others.
> Rather learn to see your own faults.
> Learn to make the world your own.
> No one is a stranger, my child;
> The whole world is our own."
> – *Holy Mother Shri Sharada Devi*

During these turbulent times, we want assurance, support, and security. Above all we want peace — peace in our personal lives and peace with our fellow beings. Mother, being none other than *Śrī Jagaddhātrī*, the support and nurse of the universe, has given us a potent prescription for finding peace: "I tell you one thing, if you want peace, do not find fault with others. Rather learn to see your own faults. Learn to make the world your own. No one is a stranger, my child; the whole world is your own." This was Mother's last message to a woman devotee and through that devotee to all of us. This message contains the whole of Vedanta philosophy — universalism, oneness of all beings, global outlook, all-embracing compassion, and practical advice for its realization, service, the worship of God in man. This is the way Mother lived throughout her life. Let's look at Mother's prescription closely.

"*If* you want peace" — well, we all want peace or so we claim. But are we ready to pay the price for peace? What is the significance of the preposition *if*? The word *if* implies there may

A PRESCRIPTION FOR PEACE

be a doubt whether we really want it. We should sincerely ask ourselves before we complain that we don't have it, if we really want peace of mind, if we are earnest in our determination to achieve this peace. Spiritual peace requires self-sacrifice. In *The Imitation of Christ*, Thomas à Kempis has remarked, "All men desire peace, but very few desire those things that make for peace." Shri Ramakrishna used to say that two things were necessary to find God: yearning and sincerity. This statement seems like an oversimplification; it is so straightforward. Yet Shri Ramakrishna said, "People shed bucketful of tears for their near and dear ones, but how many cry for God?" It's not that easy to have real yearning. But if we really want lasting peace, which means discovering our divinity within, and are determined in our resolve, Mother advised us not to see the faults of others.

This is a very pragmatic yet comprehensive part of Mother's prescription. The natural tendency of the mind is to externalize itself. Swami Turiyananda said that we always see others' *suṣupti*, deep sleep, never our own. Mother wisely said, "The mind is everything: It is in the mind alone that one feels pure and impure. A person, first of all, must make his own mind guilty and then alone he can see another person's guilt. Does anything ever happen if you enumerate his faults? It only injures you." Mother had deep insight into the complexities of the human mind. That is why she encouraged those wanting lasting peace to strive for it from the inside out. According to Mother the source of any trouble or problem in our lives, uncomfortable as it may be to accept, is within us. Our emotional responses are not reflecting the truth, but merely our reactions to what is happening to us or around us. If we want peace there is no power on earth that can make us peaceless. Mother said: "Everything depends on one's mind. Nothing can be achieved without purity of mind. There is evil in your mind. That is why you can't find peace. He who has a pure mind sees everything pure."

Mother taught us not so much through words as through her example. Not finding fault with others was deeply ingrained in her character. When she says that faultfinding is the obstruction to peace, she strikes at the root of peacelessness. Not seeing the faults of others doesn't mean not recognizing the limitations of others: We all have shortcomings. What Mother meant was not evaluating the person on that basis; instead we should try to see the divine within the person. Mother compassionately told a disciple, "To err is human. One must not take that into account. It is harmful for oneself. One gets into the habit of finding fault.... Do not look for faults in others, or your own eyes will become faulty." Again she warned us, "Don't hurt others' feelings. By indulging in rude words one's nature becomes rude. One's sensitivity is lost if one has no control over one's speech. And once a man casts all consideration for others to the winds, he stops at nothing." Mother is cautioning us not to allow negative thoughts to gain entry into our minds. She once remarked, "I cannot see anybody's faults. If a man does a trifle for me, I try to remember him even for that. To see the faults of others! One should never do it. I never do so. Forgiveness is *tapasyā*"[austerity].

Feel for Others

Mother had a delicate knack of dealing with erring humanity. She deeply felt for others and sympathized with them in their difficulties. Further Mother was a realist. She knew that there was no ideal situation in life — within the family (her crazy family was a handful), in work or human relationships. There is always a hitch somewhere. Perfection cannot be found in this world. Since we can't change people or circumstances, we have to change ourselves, our attitude of how we look at things. This is the way to peace. Seeing defects in everything and everyone around us doesn't change anything. If we soak our mind in the dye of others' faults, it becomes stained. Instead, if we look for others' good qualities, we will become virtuous.

In dealing with difficult, recalcitrant people Mother responded with love and compassion. She was always generous and nonjudgmental. Because she respected others and treated them with dignity, she was able to bring out their honorable qualities. A striking example is Mother's interaction with Amzad, a thief, who took refuge in Mother, doing many small jobs and errands for her. Mother has shown us, if we cultivate noble tendencies and ignore others' irritating negative qualities, peace of mind will come. Further Mother saw the divine in others, her every action was service to God in man: It was worship. She was unmindful of wayward or disreputable qualities in others because she saw the real person, the divine, beneath the qualities. This prompted her to say, "Amzad is as much my son as Sharat (Swami Saradananda) is."

There are countless incidents in Mother's life when in spite of rude, outrageous behavior she patiently did whatever was needed for the other person's good. She never condemned others or heeded others' criticism or gossip. No matter how much she was inconvenienced or insulted, she never took it personally: She always excused or overlooked reprehensible behavior. At the same time she didn't condone immoral or unethical actions, but she had her own way of changing the tendencies of the person. She remarked to someone: "Suppose one of my children has smeared himself with dirt. It is I, and no one else, who shall have to wash him clean and take him in my arms. To make mistakes is man's very nature; but few of those who criticize know how to correct them." Once when some people of questionable character brought some fruit for offering, members of her household objected. Mother scolded, "I know who is good and who is bad." Again she would say, "I am the mother of the wicked, as I am the mother of the virtuous." Mother always magnified good qualities, even if slight. She never made people feel small. On the contrary all felt elevated and full of worth as her child. It was as if Mother lived in a world made up entirely of her own children.

Next, Mother says, "Don't find fault with others. Rather learn to see your own faults." This introspection is essential according to Mother to assess where we stand. Though we all have shortcomings, Mother wanted us to emphasize our divinity. As children of God we are perfect, but as seekers we have our limitations and acknowledging those limitations makes us humble, which in turn enables us to overcome them. But more importantly through the practice of introspection, we will find our deeper connection with God. Turning within doesn't mean shutting out people or neglecting our duties or family. On the contrary it brings complete involvement with and dedication to people and work because we recognize that all belong to God. In this way our heart can expand with selfless love; we become less inclined to see the faults of others because our focus is on God within the person. Mother's life is a perfect illustration of this.

Make the World Your Own

Mother continues, "Learn to make the whole world your own." This part of her prescription has a deep relevance in today's world. If we truly want to have peace on earth, we have to have peace among the peoples of the world, and of course, before having peace with others, we have to be peaceful within ourselves. Now more than ever compassion, sympathetic understanding, and acceptance are needed. All of us want to feel validated as human beings; we want to feel that we have some worth, some purpose. Mother advised us to feel for others, to identify with them, extending the rights and privileges that we expect for ourselves. She implores us, "Learn to make" which implies effort; we have to work at it. Making the whole world our own is based on the oneness of all beings. But this truth is not readily apparent to us now. We have to assert the truth, to be willing to take chances, make mistakes, and try again. If the world is our own, then we are intimately connected with all beings in an all-embracing universal brotherhood, which brings mutual love, respect, and harmony. By saying, "No one is a stranger." Mother has removed all the artificiality that separates us. She is pointing out the underlying unity behind the apparent diversity; the other person is not separate from me. Fear, suspicion, hatred, exclusiveness, revenge arise in us from the selfish idea of being separate from others. The Upanishads say, "When there is perception of another, there is fear." Duality always brings fear, but when everyone is your own, where is fear, whom to fear, when you feel the interconnectedness as Mother has shown us. She didn't talk or philosophize; what she was transparently shone in her daily life. In these beautifully simple words, "No one is a stranger," we find a broad and all-encompassing outlook on human relationships, if we desire to live a truly peaceful and harmonious life. When some of the women in her household rejected British cloth, she retorted, "They are my children too. Can I afford to be partial?"

So in divine love as Mother embodied, where there is no stranger, insecurity and fear of others cease. Further, there is no favoritism or special personal attachment for anyone. This is one of the most touching and elevating aspects of Mother's character, her all-inclusive love. Everyone who came to her felt full to the brim. Her love was boundless, without borders or conditions. Unlike us, her love for one person was not diminished by her affection for another. Forgetfulness of self and loving and caring for others bring the greatest peace. Being rooted in the Self as Mother was, she loved and comforted everyone without the slightest distinction of caste, religion, country or any other consideration. Streams of people came to her — educated, uneducated, wise, foolish, wicked, good, saintly, worldly, men, women, children and some with serious problems or concerns. Whoever came to her was her child, Mother had a wonderful way of just accepting a person for what she or he was and then lifting the person up. This is how she could transform people. Her unquestioning acceptance brought out the best. Her heart was open to all, even to the most depraved: Whatever the consequences, she took them willingly as Mother. Once she said, "There is no sin left undone by some of those who come to me, but the moment they address me as 'Mother' I forget everything else and give them perhaps more than they deserve. Yet, who else will carry their burdens and bear their afflictions?" Seeing the divine in all, her love and respect extended to animals, birds, and insects as well — even to inanimate objects. Mother always gave each one its due, be it the household broom, the *āśrama* cat or cow.

This is how we learn to make the whole world our own, psychologically and spiritually. When we follow Mother's prescription for peace, our loving concern for others that we initially have to cultivate will naturally express itself through our relationships with them. She concludes the prescription, "No one is a stranger, my child; the whole world is your own." Mother reiterates and emphasizes the final assertion: "the whole world *is* your own." Mother's prescription is the essence of *Advaita Vedānta*, non-duality, in recognizing others as our own, we are asserting this truth. When this truth is actualized in our life it brings supreme peace.

Mother has demonstrated how living in the world, we can rise above it and enjoy inner peace in the midst of life's turmoil and worry, by lifting our consciousness to a higher level through our spiritual practices, especially through *japam*, repetition of the Lord's name, and prayer — in particular, prayer for others. Sending positive thoughts of love, peace and goodwill benefits not only others, but oneself as well. She said, "If you want peace now, in this life, practice the spiritual disciplines prescribed." Her prescription of peace eloquently sums up not only her own life of silent loving service, but also how she wanted us to live. Through her infinite grace Mother has given us this message so that we may find peace for ourselves and for others.

VII

Building a Culture of Peace

by *Douglas Roche*

Notre Dame Cathedral in Paris, soaring with a perfection all its own, is a magnificent religious edifice and one of the supreme masterpieces of French art. Construction of the present church, built on the ruins of its predecessors, began in 1163 during the reign of Louis VII. Generations of stonemasons, carpenters, ironsmiths, sculptors, and glaziers gradually built the foundation, the walls, the flying buttresses, vaulting, roofing, and finally the towers of the huge church. The building was not completed until 1345.

The history of Westminster Abbey in London goes back to the sixth century. The present church was begun in 1220, when Henry III started construction of the Lady Chapel. The transept, choir, the first bay of the nave, and the chapter house were not completed until late in that century. Work then came to a halt and another two centuries passed before the nave was finished.

The Holy Mosque in Makkah, the most revered place for Muslims around the world, has been expanded several times throughout history to accommodate the growing number of pilgrims for the annual Hajj. Successive Islamic regimes spared no expense or effort to dignify and honor the Mosque. The two million pilgrims who flock to the modern setting, which was completed only in 1992, benefit from the labors of those who worked on the structure over a thousand-year period.

Through many parts of the world, the grandest architectural achievements of the great cathedrals, mosques, and temples testify to the ingenuity, skill, and toil of generations of dedicated people. It took decades, sometimes a century or more, for the grandeur of each to unfold. The craftsmen who laid the stones in the foundation did not live to see the whole structure and wonder at the power of their creation. Yet if they had not done their work meticulously, day by day, to ensure that every stone was precisely secured, the rising edifice would never have withstood the passing storms. That they would never see the end result of their work did not matter. They had seen the design, they knew a step-by-step process was required, and they believed that every small detail of their work had value.

So, too, building a culture of peace requires daily dedication to fulfill the vision. We must have the patience of those who labored on the great edifices, content just to participate without expecting to see the end product. Patience is not, however, a quality associated with the modern world. We live in an age of "instant everything": instant coffee, fast food, electronic communication, supersonic flight, and space travel. We insert raw steel into an assembly line and out comes an automobile. But human beings are not instant anything. And neither are we robots.

The incessant violence of the ages has programmed us to think of wars as the inevitable outcome of conflict. We are defensive and suspicious of others, the adaptation of human beings — to change images of the enemy into understanding and tolerance, to replace armaments with disarmament, to stop exploiting the weak and the environment, and to practice sustainable development — takes a long time.

The time required to educate and transform sufficient number of individuals so that they embrace the culture of peace conflicts with the necessity of getting the job done now. The trend lines of population growth, resource scarcities, the rising demands of the oppressed, and the proliferation of weapons of mass destruction mean that we are dealing with a finite window of opportunity to resolve world issues. How then do we reconcile

BUILDING A CULTURE OF PEACE

the fact that human beings cannot be reprogrammed instantly with the new urgencies of the culture of peace? This question can lead to an agonizing of the human spirit, and then perhaps to a lapse into lethargy. The great virtues of faith, hope, and love have never been needed so much as they are needed now to cope with the challenge confronting us.

Certainly, the complexities of our time defy a simple answer, let alone the formulation of one policy for all. Still, the list of 50 Ways to Build World Peace shows how an individual can approach large issues by small and meaningful actions, "Teaching your children about peace" and "aiding the starving" are not only achievable today, but can have a profound effect on the future. The list of 50 Ways may appear to suggest simple actions, but they are certainly not simplistic.

Fifty Ways to Build World Peace

Take your share of responsibility for the world
Send letters to newspapers
Welcome strangers
Be friends with your neighbors
Write to world leaders
Avoid blaming others
Mediate a conflict
Smile at people when you're walking
Start a petition
Seek mutual understanding
Take action!
Aid the starving
Live simply so all can simply live
Instead of fighting, forgive
Create a world for grandchildren
Teach your children about peace
Learn new ways
Stand up against bullying

DOUGLAS ROCHE

Join peace protests
Help those in need
Educate others
Exercise tolerance
Meditate
Cultivate inner peace
Talk about peace
Know that your actions matter!
Wear a peace badge
Help provide what's missing
Protest at arms sales
Campaign against war
Write to local politicians
Share what you have
Care for your environment
Organize a peace rally
Support hunger charities
Have a loving attitude
Do voluntary service overseas
Become an activist
Speak up for peace
Think positively
Participate
Aim so everyone wins
Be open-minded
Listen before you react to anger
Consider others
Actively support peace initiatives
Exchange ideas
Help others be heard
Believe that you can make a difference
Speak out against prejudice
– Laurie Phillips
International Community Action, UK
Used with Permission

To have continuing effect, the unleashing of human energy called for by this list must be anchored in three fundamental ways that can move society from a culture of war to a culture of peace. We must understand, participate, and communicate.

Understand

When we fully understand the meaning of the photo of the Earth sent back by astronauts — in which we see this beautiful, fragile sphere as a whole — an attitudinal change occurs. Though we continue to live on the streets of our own community, the image of the entire planet lifts up our thinking. Who are the people on the other side of the globe? What are they doing? What is their daily life like? This awakening to the concerns of others leads us into the sources of vast amounts of information now available about food, water, health, jobs, and other human problems faced by those in different societies. This information, available from a vast network of UN sources, leads us further into the zones of intolerance, discrimination, conflicts, and wars. Questions follow — why is there so much starvation when there is so much food in the world? Why do we tolerate the existence of nuclear weapons, which threaten to destroy the processes of life? Why are we polluting the atmosphere and waters when we have the technology to avoid this? Why do we have the UN and then refuse to empower it to stop wars and end starvation?

The first sign of real knowledge is to examine the quality of the questions it evokes. In previous centuries, we were not able to frame questions large enough to address fully the nature of the human condition. While there have always been visionaries, many of whom made the scientific and technological breakthroughs that allowed the astronauts to take the photo of the Earth, the public as a whole did not share in visionary thinking. The ordinary person has always been caught up in the mundane tasks of daily existence. What concerns our family and our business this week, not the state of the global community 25 years from now, has monopolized our attention. But now the flow of information, electronically conveyed, opens up new vistas for everyone. Many still live within the confines of their own "world" but many more now extend their thinking about the world to places far beyond their neighborhood. The questions posed by this larger view, held by growing numbers of the public, are a sign of the change in attitudes that is occurring. This new attitude is the first requisite of a culture of peace.

Participate

I referred in Chapter 9 [author's book, *The Human Right to Peace*] to the emergence of the new civil society. This is truly one of the great phenomena of our time. If people who belonged to NGOs once felt on the margins of the decision-making processes, civil society now effectively injects itself into public policy debates. The rate of participation is a direct corollary of the flow of information. "Smart mobs" are the twenty-first century vehicle for people power. The combination of a world attitude developed by flows of information and the number of people involved in the new forms of social interaction is a power the world (and certainly the politicians) has not seen before.

Many politicians are worried about the state of democracy because of declining voter turnout at elections. They are missing the point. Many, particularly the young, are bypassing the traditional political processes precisely because they are so antiquated and incapable of solving contemporary security problems. The more direct actions of civic involvement — to express one's opinion and link with like-minded individuals across the globe — are more appealing. Today, democracy does not equal political involvement. That is a huge change in thinking that I myself have witnessed during 30 years in public life. Democracy is thriving as never before.

The "hierarchy" of political direction is coming to end, if it is not already finished. The trouble President George W. Bush had in getting his war against Iraq started illustrates that leaders, no matter how powerful, can no longer just commit entire societies to war. The power of people, who now understand the measures available to resolve conflicts in a fair and just manner without violence, has asserted itself. That it did not win the day on the Iraq issue does not deny the increasing influence of civil society in shaping the future. Again, this bodes well for the development of a culture of peace.

Communicate

Understanding and participation inevitably lead to communication. Communicating is what we constantly do now. Marshall McLuhan may have been right a generation ago when he said: "The medium is the message." But he would have to update his aphorism today. The message now uses the medium. I do not refer to the mainline media, which, like the political structure, is still locked in a corporate mentality that regards the public as nothing more than avaricious, mentally deficient consumers. The mainline media thrive on confrontation, whether in fiction or real life, and cunningly feed the baser instincts we all have. Mainline media outlets are not as important anymore to those who have discovered the powers of alternate communication, from the cell phone to text messaging. The Internet is the centerpiece of the revolution in electronic communication. It is the base of new ways of receiving information, from UN documents to chat rooms where social activists converge.

The Internet is not the message. The message is that we no longer need the mainline media to inform us about what is going on in the world. Civil society has a message and employs the new medium to transmit knowledge on a mass scale — knowledge that is unfiltered by editors who have the interests of their own medium largely in mind as they make daily decisions about what we will see or read. People highly knowledgeable in the elements of the culture of peace have a hard time getting access to the mainline media, but the specialists in the culture of war are seen all the time. The mainline media, still treat war as an adventure. Alternative media delve into the creativity required for peace. In the new medium, peace is explained widely; war is criticized.

This does not mean that advocates of the culture of peace should ignore the mainline media. Quite the reverse. They should send letters to the editor, contribute articles for the op-ed pages, phone radio call-in shows, and express their views in the polls increasingly done by media. They should, in short, seek to balance the war coverage with peace coverage. They need to speak up so that editors learn that there are significant sections of the audience who want to hear about the important themes of peace. Often the knowledge gained from alternative sources is the factor that enables and emboldens individuals to speak out publicly.

Not Seeing the Blossom

This book is premised on the belief — which the UN has stated — that the peoples of the world have a sacred right to peace. We must insist on this truth and let no one dissuade us from it by the false claims of "impracticability." Nothing is more practical. Gandhi showed the power of non-violent resistance to social injustice. The time has come to resist the greatest social injustice — the institution of war. For war will kill us all. The only way humanity can survive is by overcoming the culture of war, which has brought us to the unacceptable state of now being the authors of our own destruction.

If, in previous times, it could be said that humanity did not possess the tools of peace but only the tools of war, that condition no longer exists. The UN gives us the base of international law to resolve human conflict. No government or group can any longer legitimately employ the old concept of a "just war" in pursuit of its goals.

We have not yet reached sufficient maturity of civilization to enforce the right to peace. Governments, at least some of them, are still too strong and are able to overcome the wishes of those who have turned against war. But this situation will not prevail forever. It will give way to those who demand the right to peace, just as the forces of slavery, colonialism, and apartheid gave way when the opposition became strong enough. That is why developing the elements of a culture of peace — education, sustainable development, respect for all human rights, equality between men and women, democratic participation, understanding and tolerance, free flow of information, and human security for all — is so important. A culture of peace will not only make the world a more human place; it will lead inexorably to the acquisition of the human right to peace. Future generations, when they have tasted the fruit of a culture of peace, will recognize almost intuitively that peace is their right. They will demand it. Our role, as the twenty-first century begins, is to nourish the seeds of peace so that the blossom appears.

The full blossom may not appear until my grandchildren, or their grandchildren, have grown up. I accept the prospect that I will not see the blossom. The immediate goal is for every generation to ensure that there will be a following generation. The advance of civilization thus far tells me that humanity is not fated for oblivion; indeed, the new interconnected human community is a source of strength to continue building the culture of peace. I must feel this strength so that I can talk and write, in realistic terms, of achieving the human right to peace. I do feel the strength. The strength of this moment gives me hope for the future, and hope is itself a powerful motivation for action. This hope for a decent future for humanity must awaken a universal sense of responsibility. When "we the peoples" seize this responsibility, the human right to peace will be assured.

VIII

Peacemaking

by Eknath Easwaran

> Blessed are the peacemakers, for they shall be called the children of God. *Sermon on the Mount*

"Peace," according to Spinoza, "is not an absence of war. It is a virtue, a state of mind, a disposition for benevolence, trust, and justice." From this one quotation, you can see how far beyond politics the mystics' definition of peace goes. If peace would only be approached as "a virtue, a disposition," the balance of terror in which most nations on earth hang would soon vanish. Arms limitation treaties are a necessary first step; but even if all weapons were to disappear from the earth, Spinoza might tell us today, that would not guarantee peace. We must actively cultivate peace as a virtue, trying to make it a permanent state of mind.

Good people around the globe today are concerned about taking the external steps necessary to promote peace, but if we want a lasting solution we must search deeper, into this largely ignored dimension within ourselves. If we acknowledge the relevance of this dimension, we can hope to do away with war; if we continue to ignore it, no external measure can be of lasting help.

There is a vital connection, the mystics assure us, between the peace or violence in our minds and the conditions that exist outside. When our mind is hostile, it sees hostility everywhere, and we act on what we see. If we could somehow attach a monitor to the mind, we would see the indicator swing into a red danger zone, whenever consciousness is agitated by forces like anger and self-will. Acting in anger is not just the result of an agitated mind; it is also a cause, provoking retaliation from others and further agitation in our own mind. If negative behavior becomes habitual, we find ourselves chronically in a negative frame of mind and continually entangled in pointless conflicts — just the opposite of peaceful and pacifying.

"A disposition for benevolence." What a remarkable psychologist is this Spinoza! Millions of people get angry every day over trifles; when this goes on and on, the mind develops a disposition for anger. It doesn't really need a reason to lose its temper; anger is its chronic state. But we should never look on angry people as inherently angry. They are simply people whose minds have been conditioned to get angry, usually because they cannot get their own way. Instead of benevolence, they have developed a habit of hostility. For peace, Spinoza tells us, we need only turn that habit around.

In order to do effective peace work, to reconcile individuals, communities, or countries, we have to have peace in our mind. If we pursue peace with anger and animosity, nothing can be stirred up but conflict. In the end, the tide of violence we see rising day by day can be traced not to missiles or tanks but to what builds and uses those missiles and tanks: the minds of individual men and women. There is where the battle for peace has to be won. As the UNESCO constitution puts it, "Since war is born in the minds of men, it is in the minds of men that we have to erect the ramparts of peace." A familiar truth, but one we still have not learned.

How can peace ever emerge from actions prompted by suspicion, anger, and fear? By their very nature, such actions provoke retaliation in kind. If Mahatma Gandhi were here to look behind the scenes at our international summit meetings and accords, he would say compassionately, "Yes, these are a good beginning, but you need to follow them up. You're sitting at a peace table, but there is no peace in your hearts."

I knew hundreds of students in India during Gandhi's long struggle for independence from the British Empire. I met hundreds more in Berkeley during the turbulent sixties, when students all over the country were honestly trying to work for peace. I watched their relationships with one another, especially with those who differed with them, and I saw that these relationships often were not harmonious. If your mind is not trained to make peace at home, Gandhi would ask, how can you hope to promote peace on a larger scale? Until we develop enough mastery over our thinking process to maintain a peaceful attitude in all circumstances — a "disposition for benevolence" — we are likely to vacillate when the going gets tough, without even realizing what has happened.

After some of those demonstrations that were capturing headlines, I used to remind my friends that agitating for peace and actually bringing it about are not necessarily the same. Stirring up passions, provoking animosity, and polarizing opposition may sometimes produce short-term gains, but it cannot produce long-term beneficial results because it only clouds minds on both sides. Progress comes only from opening others' eyes and hearts, and that can happen only when people's minds are calmed and their fears allayed. It is not enough if your political will is peaceful; your entire will should be peaceful. It is not enough if one part of your personality says, "No more war"; the whole of your personality should be non-violent.

One of these students told me with chagrin that he once found himself using his fists to promote peace. Things just got out of control. "How did that happen?" he asked incredulously. "I never would have dreamed of doing such a thing!"

I told him not to judge himself too harshly: After all, the will to strike back is part of our biological heritage. When push comes to shove, unless we have trained ourselves to harness our anger — to put it to work to heal the situation instead of aggravating it — it is monumentally difficult for most of us to resist the impulse to retaliate.

PEACEMAKING

In situations like these, one first aid measure is to leave the scene and take a mantram walk. The force of your anger will drive the mantram deeper, bringing you closer to the day when you can rise above those fierce negative forces. Each repetition of the mantram, especially in trying moments, is like money put into a trust account in the Bank of Saint Francis. One day that account will mature, and you will become an instrument of peace. You may have no idea of what capacity you will serve in: After all, Francis himself hadn't a clue to the direction his life would take when he began placing stone upon stone to restore the chapel at San Damiano. But you can be sure that the banker within will provide you with enough compassion, security, and wisdom to make a creative contribution to solving the problems of our times.

The mystics are tremendous psychologists. It has taken more than two thousand years for secular civilization to begin to accept that penetrating aphorism of Ruysbroeck, which expresses a central tenet of spiritual psychology: "We behold that which we are, and we are that which we behold." If we have an angry mind, we will see life as full of anger; if we have a suspicious mind, we will see causes for suspicion all around: Precisely because we and the world are not separate.

When suspicion lurks in our hearts, we can never quite trust others. Most of us go about like medieval knights, carrying a shield wherever we go in case we have to ward off a blow. After a day of carrying a shield around at the office, who wouldn't be exhausted? We take the shield to bed with us for seven or eight hours and wake up wondering why we still feel worn out. And of course, with a big piece of iron on one arm, we find it hard to embrace a friend or offer a hand in help. What began as a simple defense mechanism becomes a permanent, crippling appendage.

Statesmen are no different: They too are human beings, albeit with a most important job. When they go to the conference table, they too carry their shields. Worse, their suspicions may prompt them to carry a sword in the other hand, or to sit down with a clenched fist, which as Indira Gandhi once said, makes it impossible to shake hands. Yet that is just how most nations today come to the peace table, desiring a meeting of minds but prepared to fight to get their own way. They don't expect peace, they expect trouble: and expecting trouble, I sometimes think, is the best way of inviting it.

Changing Our Way of Seeing

When we change our way of seeing, we begin to live in a different world. If we approach others with respect and trust, with a great deal of patience and internal toughness, we will slowly begin to find ourselves in a compassionate universe where change for the better is always possible, because of the core of goodness we see in the hearts of others. That is how I see the world today. It is not that I fail to see suffering and sorrow. But I understand the laws of life and see its unity everywhere, so I feel at home wherever I go.

Wernher von Braun, the pioneer of astronautics, once said that for those who know its laws, outer space is not the hostile environment it seems but very friendly. Traveling in space is as safe as sitting in our living rooms — so long as we understand the rules of space and abide by them. Similarly, those who know the laws of the mind live in peace and security even in the midst of storms. They choose not to hate because they know that hatred only breeds hatred, and they work for peace because they know that preparation for war can only lead to war. When people wonder if programs like "Star Wars" will work, I reply, "That is the last question we should ask. The first question is, can wrong means ever lead to right ends?" Can we ever prepare for war and get peace?

"One day," said Martin Luther King, Jr., "we must come to see that peace is not merely a distant good but a means by which we arrive at that good. We must pursue peaceful ends through peaceful means." In his speech accepting the Nobel Peace Prize in 1964, King said:

> Nonviolence is the answer to the crucial political and moral questions of our time; the need for man to overcome oppression and violence without resorting to oppression and violence. Man must evolve for all human conflict a method which rejects revenge, aggression, and retaliation. The foundation of such a method is love.

It is a living law, a law governing all of life, that ends and means are indivisible. Right means cannot help but lead to right ends; and wrong means — waging war, for example, to ensure peace — cannot help but result in wrong ends. Gandhi went to the extent of telling us to use right means and not worry about the outcome at all; the very laws of our existence will ensure that the outcome of our efforts will be beneficial in the long run. The only question we have to ask ourselves is: Am I giving everything I can to bring about peace — at home, on the streets, in this country, around the world? If enough of us start acting on this question, peace is very near.

What we do with our hands, the mystics say, is a direct expression of the forces in our minds. Even our technology is an expression of some of our deepest desires. The crisis of industrial civilization, which could create the conditions of paradise on this earth and yet threatens to destroy it, only reflects the deeper division in our hearts. "Our nuclear buildup isn't something unique," says Joseph Chilton Pearce, an author and former humanities teacher, "but it is the clearest and most inescapable end result, or final expression, of our whole current mode of life and way of thinking." Instead of blaming our problems on some intrinsic flaw in human nature, we must squarely take responsibility for our actions as human beings capable of rational thought.

Taking Responsibility

But this view has a heartening side: If it is we who got ourselves into this habit of suspicion, we have the capacity to get ourselves out too. Simply to understand this is a great step in the right direction, where we do not sit back and bemoan our irrational "animal" behavior but accept that our nuclear-threatened world is an expression of our way of thinking and feeling. The terrible dilemma which we face is the ultimate result of our mode of life, our motivation, the kind of relationships we have cultivated with other countries, our whole philosophy of life. Here again is Martin Luther King, Jr.:

> I refuse to accept the idea that the "isness" of man's present nature makes him morally incapable of reaching up for the "oughtness" that forever confronts him. ...
> I refuse to accept the cynical notion that nation after nation must spiral down a militaristic stairway into the hell of nuclear destruction. I believe that unarmed truth and unconditional love will have the final word in reality.

In this presumably sophisticated world, it is considered naive to be trusting. In that case I am proud to say that I must be one of the naivest people on earth. If someone has let me down a dozen times, I will still trust that person for the thirteenth time. Trust is a measure of your depth of faith in the nobility of human nature, of your depth of love for all. If you expect the worst from someone, the worst is what you will usually get. Expect the best and people will respond: Sometimes swiftly, sometimes not so swiftly, but there is no other way.

When statesmen and politicians view other nations through the distorting lens of hatred and suspicion, the policies they come up with only keep the fires of hostility smoldering. "Hate those who hate us — and, if possible, threaten them as well": This is scarcely a path to peace; it is only the path of stimulus and response. Jesus gave us a path that matches means to ends: "Do good to them that hate you." This should be the basis even of foreign policy. There is no surer route to building trust and dispelling fear, the prime mover behind all arms races.

Because we see as we are, not only are our policies backward but our priorities are upside down. We long for peace but work for war, often under the label of "defense." That is where

PEACEMAKING

the time, talent, and resources of some of our "best and brightest" go. Joseph Chilton Pearce again is direct and to the point:

> From where does our incredibly sophisticated arsenal of destruction come? From the Pentagon? They couldn't make a paper airplane. Our instruments of destruction come from our "finest intellects" — the academic scientific community who, with one side of their mouth, bemoan the stupid politicians, and with the other, beg for DOD [Department of Defense] grants, money, fame and Nobels, by which they give the "warlords" their swords. Withdraw the supporting think-systems from Harvard, M.I.T., U. Cal, Stanford, Caltech, and so on, and the power of the warlords would disappear.

Being a scientist is a tremendous responsibility. If just half a dozen top scientists from institutions like these should withdraw their support from the war effort, it would be a great contribution to peace. Instead, some of our best scientific thinking and technological talent stays with war. No one has appraised the result better than General Omar Bradley, whom I quoted at the beginning of this book. He says:

> We have grasped the mystery of the atom and rejected the *Sermon on the Mount*. ... The world has achieved brilliance without conscience. Ours is a world of nuclear giants and ethical infants. We know more about war than we do about peace, more about killing than we know about living.

Strong words, but we need a strong reminder of how ridiculous our values have become. General Bradley's language reminds me of an episode I once saw in a run-of-the-mill Indian movie, in which a simple villager goes to Bombay for the first time. When he comes back, his friends ask him what he thought of the big city. "Such tall buildings," he says, "and such small people." Very perceptive. That is our world, "nuclear giants and ethical infants."

When I first arrived in this country, at the Port of New York, friends took me to Times Square to ooh and aah at the architecture. I went, but I didn't ooh and aah. That puzzled them. "Oh, you're just acting blasé," they said. "You know you've never seen a skyscraper before. Aren't you impressed?"

"Buildings don't impress me," I confessed. "People do. I may not have seen a skyscraper, but I have met and walked with a man to match the Himalayas, Mahatma Gandhi. Show me someone big like that and you'll see how impressed I can be."

Do you remember the movie in which Charlie Chaplin goes on looking for the top of a skyscraper until finally he topples over backward? That is not going to happen to me, and it should not happen to you. We should never be impressed by something just because it is big, whether it is a big building or a big bomb. These are not the signs of an advanced civilization, and they have nothing to do with progress and growth. One real "ethical giant" is of much more significance in history.

I believe it was Prince Edward, the Duke of Windsor, who went on a shooting expedition when visiting India many years ago and managed to get separated from the rest of his party. Finally the others started firing into the air to make their position known. "Ah!" Edward exclaimed when he heard the shots. "The sound of civilization!"

Today, instruments of destruction have become so deadly that however sophisticated the technology, nations that concentrate on developing, selling, and stockpiling weapons might be said to be losing their claim to civilization. We can make a rough map of the truly civilized world: The bigger the arsenal of nuclear weapons, the weaker the claim to being a civilized power. To be truly civilized, a government must subscribe to the highest law: Respect for life, to the point of being willing to kill or to cause others to kill.

Making Peace a Reality

I am a very hard-nosed person. I do not get impressed by speeches, rallies and media coverage about arms control. How much are we willing to give, and give up, to make peace a reality? That is the question. It is not just what we say and write but how we order our lives — how we apportion our time, distribute our resources, and behave in everyday relationships — that counts for peace. "We rage against 'forces' over which we have no control," Pearce says. "But control would require effort, and our efforts go to self-comfort, personal benefit, and living the good life."

"I see no way out of this dilemma," says the veteran statesman George Kennan, who has lived through thaws and freezes in the Cold War since 1945, "other than by a bold and sweeping departure, a departure that would cut surgically through the exaggerated anxieties, the self-indentured nightmares, and the sophisticated mathematics of destruction in which we have all been entangled over these recent years, and would permit us to move with courage and decision to the heart of the problem."

Kennan is talking about nothing less than a complete reversal of our ways of thinking. Both Washington and Moscow peer out on the world through a curtain of suspicion, mistrust, and fear which distorts vision and allows no other way of seeing. How can peace ever come in such a climate? To have peace we must learn to see where we stand on common ground, beginning with certain basic truths: That people in all countries are essentially the same, whether their governments are communist or capitalist, and that neither of the superpowers threatens the other as much as the arms race threatens us all.

To change course like this, we human beings have to learn to talk to each other even when our opinions differ. And that requires respect. Nothing closes communication more swiftly and effectively than this business of painting the other side with an all-black brush. If it were not so tragic, it would be amusing to compare how often the same comments are hurled like rockets by both sides. Each claims to be innocent of all wrong and views the other as the epitome of evil.

Citizen exchanges can do wonders to dissolve such barriers on the personal level. It pleases me very much to see that high school and university exchange programs are beginning to include teachers and students from China and the Soviet Union. We can send more students, more scholars, more artists and dancers and musicians and athletes, to countries with whom we differ politically; they do more for peace than most politicians. It is more than a quarter of a century since I first came to this country on the Fulbright exchange program as a professor of English literature, and I feel I am still fulfilling the spirit of my exchange. I still work for international peace — not by giving lectures on a few dusty texts, but by dispelling mistrust and suspicion in every way I can.

Rich or poor, powerful or not so powerful, ally or antagonist or nonaligned, every nation needs help and understanding if the world is to get out of this nuclear trap, for nuclear arms are no longer exclusive to superpowers. We must begin to see this massive threat as an opportunity to build a new world — one world, not divided by nationalistic rivalries — or else we shall perish by our own politics.

This is an opportunity for every one of us. Our children face right now the dreadful reality that life as we know it can he wiped out in half an hour's time. If we remember this always, it will bring the motivation to work hard for our children, for their life, for their world.

Our children deserve to grow up in a peaceful world, and it is our responsibility to do everything we can to see that they get the chance. This is why our schools are so important — and let me repeat; the home is the most important school of all. Teachers should not have to declare themselves "educators for social responsibility"; that is their role. I want to see that hundreds of millions of children understand this basic choice and have the opportunity to make it. When they reach voting age they should be able to tell anyone running for office, "If you support war, you are not going to get my vote. You must stand squarely and unequivocally for peace; then I'll see that you get in." If enough of us say that and mean it, the struggle is as good as won.

One very serious obstacle to children growing up with this point of view was pointed out a few years ago on the front page of the *Christian Science Monitor* during the Christmas shopping season. The headline read, "Toy Companies Ride Military Wave and Watch Kids Catch It." How early the seeds of violence are sown! Toys are not neutral; they influence children's thinking and emotions, for better or worse. When my young friend Christina was two, she used to bring her dolls with her to the dinner table. When I asked her, "How is your little one today?" she would say, "She has a cold." "Does she wake you up by crying at night?" "No, she just sleeps." Those dolls were real to her. Children need toys that are fun, but they also need toys that inspire them, toys that make them more sensitive to other people and creatures. So many toys today do just the opposite.

The *Monitor* article went on to supply illustrations: "Tricycles with bazookas attached; guns that shoot beams of infrared light at the opponent. Dolls with bad breath, or those with controversial messages, like Grace, the pro life doll, and Nomad the Arab terrorist. These and other toys are on more wishlists than ever before." Children cannot be held responsible for putting violent, tawdry stuff on their Christmas lists. It is we adults who are responsible: Well-intentioned parents, grandparents, relatives, and friends; television programmers and media manipulators; and especially those who make and sell whatever promises to bring in a profit, regardless of the values it may represent.

Every parent can play a useful role in reversing this trend — particularly every mother. When you give toys to children, or allow them to buy them for themselves, you have to consider that you are not just giving them something to entertain them; you are giving them an instrument that may influence their thinking and living for decades.

Of course, big money is involved in toys today. Isn't it involved in most of our big problems? "Controversy" over such toys, the *Monitor* continues, "has not hurt sales. Laser Tag, which is number five on *Toy and Hobby World* magazine's most-popular lists, is expected to bring in a hundred million in sales this year." (Laser Tag involves shooting at opponents with a light-gun; when a person is hit, his target gives off an electronic death rattle.) That is a hundred million from the pockets of parents. The president of the company that makes Laser Tag says that the toy merely puts a high-tech spin on a time-honored game. "Laser Tag", he says, "is a vehicle to bring children together." It brings them together in insensitivity to violence, and it fosters the thinking that perpetuates war.

Developments like these will bear bitter fruit in the lives of our children, and that is why every parent has a responsibility to think about this issue, write about it, and speak about it to others. I admit, this is un-dramatic work. Nobody is likely to give you recognition or put you on the front page of the newspaper. But this is the kind of work that expresses real commitment to peace. If a thousand or so mothers and fathers speak up on this issue, within ten years we will see a completely different kind of toy market in this country. Toys that help, inspire, and strengthen while they entertain are quite within human reach.

But the surest way to educate children for peace is through our personal example. This is the responsibility of every one of us — not just parents, but everyone who has contact with young people. Children quietly absorb what we teach through our actions and attitudes, so there is no more powerful way to show them what the silent power of a peaceful mind and a loving heart can do.

One of the things that impressed me deeply about Gandhi, for example, was his ability to calm a violent crowd. I don't think anywhere in this country are you likely to see crowds like those in India. You got an idea of them in the film *Gandhi*: Tens of thousands of people gathered in one place; and in those days they were sometimes in no mood to be nonviolent. Often Gandhi stood before an angry crowd clamoring for retaliation, "an eye for an eye." I have seen him quiet them just by raising his hand, and with one reminder make them stop to think: "An eye for an eye only makes the whole world blind." After a few minutes we would all go away calmer and braver, having tasted a little of the peace that was in the heart of this spiritual giant. The eyes, the voice, and the gestures of such a person communicate with people even from a distance and bring them peace.

We may not be called on to face multitudes or to calm the storms of nations, but we can all begin by calming storms in the teacup of our homes. This is the only way we can help our children to grow up in peace and security. We may not have found a world at peace ourselves, but it is quite within our power to create one for the next generation — if we will only make peace, rather than personal profit or pleasure, the first priority in our lives.

Family relationships are so important that we cannot afford to relegate them to secondary status, putting children or partner after our job and income and status. Nothing is more important than the children of our nation, our only essential resource; and each of us, remember, is their teacher by our example. Every morning after meditation I ask myself what I would be without my grandmother, my spiritual teacher, I might have acquired a well-trained intellect, but I would never have learned how to train my mind, the most precious skill on earth.

IX

Peace: Oneness with God

by Jonathan Roof

[From the teachings of Sathya Sai Baba]

Peace is like a well-channeled river. It does not rest in a static state; rather, it harmoniously adapts to change. Although a river constantly flows, it maintains equilibrium with the shore. From obscure mountain origins, it plunges to the plains, assuming a name, and then it merges namelessly in the vast ocean. Peace also flows and grows; it is the sign of God's creation working in harmony.

Peace for spiritual aspirants is a state of equanimity based on understanding of and adherence to *dharma* (spiritual duty). When we understand the divine basis for creation and live in accordance with it, we can move unruffled by the currents of daily events. Recognition of divinity in all creatures and all objects grants us courage and confidence. When we lead virtuous lives, leaving the results of our actions to God, we experience peace.

> When man thinks, speaks, and acts along virtuous lines, his conscience will be clean and he will have inner peace. Knowledge is power, it is said; but virtue is peace. *Sathya Sai Speaks* 10, p. 267

To experience peace, we must master our unreasonable expectations. Agitation usually results from unfulfilled desires, not from external conditions. The mind creates wrong desire when it loses control over the senses. Virtue requires us to hold the senses in check. If we hold to material values, we lose our inner peace. If we live virtuously, we grow into unbounded joy.

> What exactly is peace? It is the stage in which the senses are mastered and held in balance. *Sanathana Sarathi*, Jan. 1985, p.11

A controlled mind enables us to rest, content with the present, not dwelling on the past or expecting too much from the future. When the endless progression of thoughts is controlled, the divine purity of consciousness shines forth. The mind should be a tool of the *Ātmā*, the inner divinity. The mind should not become our master, roaming unchecked among the objects of desire. The mind creates desire, so it must be taught to remain quiet when it is not required for a specific task. Like a small child, it must be taught to limit its reach and to rest occasionally.

> There is some small confusion of terms, for there is no mind as such. The mind is a web of desires. Peace of mind is no desires, and in that state there is no mind. Mind is destroyed, so to speak. Peace of mind really means purity, complete purity of consciousness. *Conversations*, p. 44

Our Real Nature

A tiger cub was once separated from its mother and lost in the forest. It happened to come upon a gathering of goats and joined them for companionship. After some time, the cub began to eat grass and behave like the goats with which it lived. It bleated and pranced just like the others. This went on for months, until the herd was spied by the mother tigress. She pounced upon the group, scattering them in all directions. The young tiger cub bleated and dashed for cover in panic. However, the tigress noticed the incongruous "goat" and chased it down.

Dragging the terrified cub to a water hole, she instructed it to look into the water. The cub was amazed to find that he looked just like the fearsome tigress, not the goats with which he had associated. He was, after all, a master of the forest himself.

We tend to be grass-eating tigers. We have come to believe that we are something less than divinity. If we look into the pool of spiritual truth, we find that we are the very source of wisdom, love, and peace. When we still the mind, it will cease to delude us into believing that we are less than what we are — the *Ātmā*.

Ātmika peace is our true nature; it is acquired when we look within. If we are concerned only with outer circumstances, the jumble of daily events, we will be unable to experience peace. Ignorance of our divine origin causes us to be elated or dejected at the changing course of events. Our true nature is selfless love and joyful peace, unbounded by time or circumstance. It manifests when it is allowed to shine through the clouds of illusion.

> Once you enter the depths of the sea, it is all calm, it is all peace. Agitation, noise, confusion — all are only on the outer layers. So also in the innermost recesses of the heart, there is a reservoir of *śānti* (peace) where you must take refuge. *Sathya Sai Speaks* 1, p. 172.

The possibility of acquiring inner peace is not so distant as we may think. In fact, all people possess it already. Peace is our essential nature, but it is hidden by the clouds of attachment. Peace is like the sun, always shining, but temporarily covered by the darkness of anger or selfishness. The divine self, the *Ātmā*, radiates peace and joy. We need only to look within for the source of our joy.

> Peace and joy can be secured only by realizing that they are one's own real nature. *Sathya Sai Speaks* 6, p. 58

Inner Peace: Outer Peace

Faith results in a peaceful outlook. As rose-colored glasses turn everything that color, inner peace sets our own "world" at peace. When we discern the divine basis for creation, we cease to be upset by changing circumstances. Faith in God and faith in oneself set one's world at rest.

PEACE: ONENESS WITH GOD

> So real *śānti* (peace) is to be had only in the depths of the spirit, in the discipline of the mind, in faith in the one base of all this seeming multiplicity. When that is secured, it is like having gold: You can have any variety of ornaments made from it. *Sathya Sai Speaks* 1, p. 124

When we wear comfortable shoes, even the bumpiest roads seem smooth. Although the track may be covered with small stones or glass, we can walk without fear. Wherever we travel, on highway or trail, we are assured of a smooth journey. Peace within protects us in the same way. Inner peace reflects outwardly as peace in our own immediate world. What we perceive in our surroundings is a reflection of our inner state. If we realize the joy and beauty within ourselves, we also perceive it in the realm around us. Peace is a cloak which affords us comfort even on the coldest days.

> So too, the man who is at peace with himself will discern peace all around him. Nature is beauty, truth, and peace. Man sees it ugly, false, and violent that is all. *Sathya Sai Speaks* 9, p. 147

Peace in the world depends on peace in each individual. No laws or treaties can bring about peace without righteousness in individuals. Righteousness results when individuals master their unreasonable desires. With proper understanding, they leave the results of action to God and act in accordance with their spiritual duty.

> If there is righteousness in the heart
> There will be beauty in the character.
> If there is beauty in the character
> There will be harmony in the home.
> When there is harmony in the home,
> There will be order in the nation.
> When there is order in the nation,
> There will be peace in the world.
> – *Sathya Sai Speaks* 7, pp. 189-190

Righteousness in the heart results from the vision of Oneness. People of all lands share the same divine status as embodiments of God. When they recognize that the same God-nature moves in each, they will respect one another. All are waves on the ocean of God, not separate from each other or from God.

> Now all things have gone up in value; man alone has become cheap. ... He has become cheaper than animals; he is slaughtered in millions without any qualm because of the terrific growth in anger, hate, and greed: He has forgotten his unity with all men, all beings, and all worlds. The contemplation of that unity alone can establish world peace, social peace, and peace in the individual. *Sathya Sai Speaks* 4, p. 287

How to Cultivate Peace

To gain a true perspective on an object, we need to move away from it. If we are too close, we are confused by its motion or the details of its appearance. When we stand on the shore, the ocean may appear angry and restless, but from space it is a calm blue pond. Our closeness — or our attachment — to objects robs us of our peace. When objects are near, mentally, emotionally, or physically, we are more likely to relate to them on an ego level. We are apt to interpret them in terms of our own personality. To cultivate peace we must move back and detach from objects.

When we calm our emotions and center ourselves within, we gain control of our minds. Peace grants us perspective for intelligent action. In fact, peace encourages many virtues. It grants divine vision, which encourages wisdom and love.

> *Śānti* (peace) is essential for sharpness of intellect. *Śānti* develops all the beneficial characteristics of man. Even farsightedness grows through *śānti*. Through that, obstacles and dangers can be anticipated and averted. *Prasanthi Vahini*, p. 12

The vision of unity is won by intense spiritual practice. Practice helps us to see God in everything and in everyone. That vision results from clearly analyzing the results of thoughts and actions. When we see the painful consequences of desires for fleeting pleasures and material acquisitions, we learn to search

PEACE: ONENESS WITH GOD

for more lasting values. Then we experience the joy and peace derived from knowing God.

> Only thoughts of God and intense love for Him bring peace. As worldly thoughts diminish, thoughts of God increase. Normally, the mind desires these worldly things all the time. As the desires are cut one by one, the peace becomes stronger. ... When there are Godly thoughts, there is peace of mind. Swami cannot give peace of mind; one has to work for it. *Conversations*, p. 22

Until the mind is stilled and peace is experienced, we must engage the mind in pure thoughts. We must have faith that God will give us our due. The Lord dispenses results in accordance with what we have earned. If we leave the results to God, we can experience peace. Centered on God, we are content with whatever may happen.

> But you cannot easily detach yourself from activity; the mind clings to some thing or other. Make it cling to God, let it do all things for God and leave the success or failure of the thing done to God, the loss and profit, the elation and dejection. Then you have the secret of *śānti* and contentment. *Sathya Sai Speaks* 4, p. 318.

PART THREE

Inner Peace

Take refuge in Him with all thy heart
By His grace thou shalt attain
Supreme Peace and the Eternal Abode.

Bhagavad Gītā 18:62

The world that constantly challenges one is more an inner world based on the unconscious structure of mind and the conscious reactions to the external objects. Therefore if a person were to be brought into an experience of peace and joy, he must find a profound adjustment and resolution within himself. In brief, the problem of world peace cannot be encountered in the outer world. It is in the human heart where it must be tackled, confronted, and resolved.

Every human being experiences the world according to his mental structure. There, the world is not the same for everyone. To a thief, the world seems filled with thieves, while to a sorrowful man, the very moon pours down a stream of agony. However to one of mystic understanding, it is experienced as a manifestation of the Divine Self — an ocean of joy surging with waves, eddies, ripples and foam.

                              Swami Jyotirmayananda

X

Peace of Mind

by Swami Tejomayananda

I cannot give you peace of mind, but I can give you some advice on how to gain peace of mind. This advice is not new. It is a tested path by generations of great people who practiced and lived it and declared it to those that followed. Their experiments verified and confirmed the validity of those teachings. If we were to follow this advice, we would certainly attain that peace which we seek but which always seems to elude us.

We experience glimpses of this peace now and then in our lives. For instance, in deep sleep when the mind is not functioning, we experience peace. Hence, we may conclude that peace means non-functioning of the mind. However this peace of "no mind" is limited to the condition of sleep. At that time it is impossible to understand how that same peace can be attained even while the mind is functioning.

There is yet another kind of experience, one that comes after the enjoyment of some pleasure. Before the pleasure is experienced, there is a lot of excitement or agitation. At the actual moment of enjoyment, we forget everything and all agitation ceases. For some time the mind becomes quiet and we experience a relative peace, until we become agitated again. Between two wars there is a period of temporary peace. When a riot takes place in a city and the police crush it, we say that an uneasy calm prevails. This is a very fragile peace that may shatter at any moment.

A religious person who goes to a temple, mosque, or a church to pray or those that sing or listen to the glories of the Lord, also experience peace but this peace also dissolves. As long as they are in the temple or in the church they are peaceful but as soon as they leave the place of worship, the same old problems arise once again.

Why does peace leave us in the midst of changing circumstances? It is only because we are seeking, searching, and struggling for it. The more we look and struggle for it, the more peace is lost. This is the paradox. We could say, "This is very nice; we will not put in any effort." Yet, if we merely give up all effort, we cannot simply sit peacefully. Giving up the struggle is no solution either.

Vedantic literature says, "Neither by not struggling nor by struggling does man attain peace; but he who knows the Truth attains it." A man of action always thinks that a sage who is sitting quietly is doing nothing; by society's standards he is useless, a mere idler. Although it may appear that the sage is sitting idle, he maintains a state of peace — which is not an easy accomplishment. His mind is calm and absorbed. We cannot say where the mind of a person in this state is, but it is certainly neither drugged nor in a stupor. This peace is a dynamic quietude, an equilibrium achieved without struggle. How then, does the sage gain this peace? We have to realize that this peace does not come from anything external. This is the fundamental secret, the most basic fact that we have to understand.

Peace is Always Present

At the moment our minds are constantly restless and agitated. We live on sensation — newspapers, novels, and movies. Naturally, while we are seeking sensation, peace eludes us; agitation and restlessness become our nature. We expect to gain peace by some external means, while agitation remains with us all the time.

The scriptures say that the truth is quite the opposite. We cannot get peace; but if we close our eyes and stop talking, peace will be there. It is not gotten or created. In fact, what we create is disturbance. It is important to recognize that before the disturbance was created, peace existed. While the disturbance is going on, peace still remains though not experienced, and when the disturbance stops, peace is evident again.

Waves rise in the water. Before the waves rise, the water is calm. When the waves rise, the water remains unchanged, and when the waves subside water remains. In the same way, peace is always present, but we ourselves create the causes for disturbance, agitation, distraction, and restlessness — and then say that we have lost that peace.

A verse from the *Bhagavad Gītā* beautifully describes the one who attains lasting peace in this life. It says, "He who lives and transacts in the world giving up desires, free from longing and craving, free from attachment, and the ego sense of I and mine, attains peace." (2:71)

It is interesting to note that the *Bhagavad Gītā* does not say what we must do but rather, what we must get rid of. What a wonderful thing — we are not implored to do something, but are assured that peace is ours if we give up these four negative tendencies.

It is these four — desire, attachment, "I-ness," and "my-ness" — that disturb us and destroy our peace. On the surface it may seem that relinquishing these four would make us inert, like stones, but the *Bhagavad Gītā* states that such a person does live and move in the world and does so more effectively. Therefore, we need to investigate the deeper meaning of these terms as used in the scriptures. The common meaning will not be sufficient if we want to understand the full significance of the verse.

Let's analyze the word "desire." Can anyone really be free of desire? A person may desire to have a glass of water, or he may express the desire to sleep. No one can be free of such desires, for such desires are merely basic needs that must be satisfied. Hence, there should be no confusion between a desire and a basic need.

All of us desire different objects. What we need to understand is that the desire is not for the objects themselves, but what they can do for us. If we wanted the objects only, then their acquisition would bring happiness, but it does not. We want objects because we want to enjoy, and the desire to enjoy is really the desire to be happy. In fact, happiness is the culmination of all of our struggles and searching. The problem is that we want happiness but we try to gain objects, mistakenly attributing happiness to them. The result is that our real desire is never fulfilled. We are constantly struggling; changing our places, objects, and relationships to gain happiness. Yet, we never think of changing ourselves.

Our physical life depends on physical things. We need food when we are hungry, and when we are cold we need warm clothing. These are our basic needs. Satisfying them may make us comfortable, but not happy. We need to clarify the difference between happiness and comfort. Comfort does not mean happiness. Nowadays, our life has become comfortable and we have become comfortably sorrowful!

A wise person gives up the desire for objects; understanding fully that what he seeks is true and lasting happiness, which he cannot get from objects. He understands that sorrow comes from a sense of incompleteness and not because of lack of objects. We however, tend to think that our sorrow will vanish if we get a particular object, or that some person will come along and make us feel complete. But then, when the relationship ends we feel devastated.

A wise person accepts life as it comes and gives up expecting lasting happiness from objects. If the nature of objects were happiness, they would universally bring happiness to everyone at all times. The nature of sugar is sweetness. It is sweet for all, at all times. But this is not the case regarding happiness in objects. However, there is no need to discard the objects; we need only correct our understanding that they will not bring lasting happiness. A wise person may desire objects, but he will never insist on the fulfillment of such desires.

If there is no happiness in the objects themselves, then what is the source of happiness? There are only two entities in this world of experience. One is the subject "I" and the other is the world of objects. If happiness is not found in the world of objects, what remains is the subject, "I." So, happiness is me, my true and essential nature; happiness is not the nature of my body, which itself is an object. This "I" is pure Consciousness, pure Existence, which illumines the inert body and makes it sentient. This pure Consciousness is all perfect, and that is my true nature. It is not something outside of myself. At the time of a beautiful or blissful experience, our eyes just naturally close with happiness. Why? It shows that the experience of bliss and happiness is not something outside; it is deep within our selves. A realized man lives with this awareness at all times.

The Nature of Desire

Once a desire arises, we cannot forget it. There is complete insistence that things must happen the way we want. As long as we have such desires, it is impossible to gain peace. We cannot even sleep properly because our mind is so riddled with desires, let alone poised enough to gain that great and permanent peace.

Another characteristic of desire is that once we have enjoyed something, we crave for it again and again. If we are itchy and make the mistake of scratching, we will find that the itching increases. The nature of desire is just like having an itch. Once we start enjoying something, there will be more and more craving and longing for it. We keep planning for those pleasures we have not yet experienced, and then after having enjoyed them, we remember them constantly and crave for them. These are the two main things that tend to disturb us when we sit for meditation or when we go to sleep. Either we continue to plan for the future, or we try to remember our past experiences.

This does not mean that we should not plan anything. It is not the day-to-day planning for our job or profession that we need to give up, but it is the planning for pleasures and remembering them that create agitation in the mind. Therefore, if we give up these two — remembering the past and planning for the future — along with correct understanding, we can experience peace beyond our imagination.

My-ness Causes Sorrow

Besides desire, the two other obstacles to attainment of peace are the sense of "I-ness" and "my-ness." The sense of "I-ness" exists with reference to the body and its activities. When I feel that this body is "I," then I naturally feel that anything belonging to the body is mine. Thereafter if I lose that object I feel sad. The sorrow exists only because I have this "my" sense. Suppose my watch is lost, will you be unhappy? No, but I will be! Suppose I give my watch to you, and then it is lost. Then losing it no longer matters to me because the sense of "my-ness" is no longer with me. As long as there is a sense of possession, the mind suffers agitation. We feel sorrow only at a loss when this sense of "my-ness" is present — when we feel something "belongs" to us.

A businessman who had lost thousands of rupees came to me once for advice. I told him that the nature of business meant profit and loss and he should have equanimity of mind in both profit and loss. He thanked me for the good advice.

After three days, when he came to me, I was upset for having lost ten rupees. He said, "Swamiji, just three days ago when I had lost ten thousand rupees, you advised me to be calm. Now you are upset at the loss of only ten rupees!"

I said, "My dear, the difference is that the ten thousand rupees were yours, but the ten rupees were mine!"

When the idea of "my-ness" is present, we suffer whether the loss is big or small. In the *Bhagavad Gītā*, Lord Krishna says, he who is free from the sense of "my-ness," has no agitation.

How can we live practically in the world without a sense of "my-ness?" It is not to be taken literally. Suppose someone asks me, "Swamiji, whose watch is this?" I cannot say that I don't know, I would say that it is mine. There is no harm in saying that as long as I realize that the watch is merely in my keeping. If a teacher says, "He is my disciple." This does not mean that the teacher has a sense of "my-ness" and therefore will have no peace. There is a practical use of the word "my." What we must avoid is the feeling of possession and our attachment to objects. For example, when I travel by plane or train, I say, "My seat number is 25A," but when I reach the destination, I do not try to take the seat with me. I accept it as mine only for the time being, but I immediately relinquish it without a thought when I leave. I do not consider it as absolutely mine. We must understand that the possessions are only in our temporary keeping. This is how we can live peacefully with people and relatives and all of the objects that we come in contact with. This is why mothers, fathers, sisters, and brothers are all called relatives, not absolutes.

Separateness and Fear

Now the question arises: How can we give up this *ahaṁkāra* or ego, because of which we are suffering? There is a very simple exercise to reduce it. Since we have this feeling that we are great — "I did this, I achieved that" — let us note down on paper what the contributing factors were, and how many people helped us to be what we are today.

Suppose I sing well. Now, for me to be a good singer, how many things were necessary? I draw two columns on the paper and note down my contributions against the contributions of others. By comparing the two my ego must disappear. First, to

PEACE OF MIND

be able to sing I must be alive and this is certainly not my doing. Secondly, I was gifted with a good voice, which is again a gift from God. Next, I received training from my teachers and other musicians; and finally, I was the recipient of great gifts of tolerance and support from family and neighbors who had to listen while I practiced! With such a perspective we can understand that there is not a single thing that we can do or create on our own. I develop the attitude that it is my privilege to serve and delight others; God has blessed me with this voice for that purpose. Abandoning any sense of doership, we become instruments in the hands of the Lord.

The sense of "I-ness" can be given up with the understanding that God gifted us with all our faculties. Nothing is ours; we should love those around us but never with the sense of "my-ness." Thus when desires of I-ness, and my-ness (the causes of all our disturbances) are not there, we will enjoy peace of mind.

Gaining Peace

Peace is not gained by any struggle or absence of struggle. It is gained by understanding the nature of what is real. By discovering and realizing the Truth, the wise man becomes peace itself. That is "the peace that passeth all understanding," that which is beyond our mind and intellect. That peace never gets disturbed. The *Bhagavad Gītā* confirms such a peaceful mind when it says, "Having gained abidance in peace such that even mountain-like sorrows do not disturb one." This peace is present even while the wise man is working. In this peace the mind is very much alive, awake, alert, vigilant, working, functioning, dealing with life and all its problems and challenges. This is *tattva niṣṭhā* the determination of the Reality. It is not achieved by running away from life nor when the mind is suspended through laziness or drugs. There is no peace through such means.

The above approach to peace and happiness is the path of inquiry. But there is another approach, the path of devotion.

One who is devoted to the Lord and has faith that an almighty, omnipresent, omnipotent Lord is taking care of everything, has no reason to get agitated.

Generally, we think that he who does not believe in the existence of God is an atheist. This is not true. He who believes in the existence of God and still says, "I am not peaceful" is really an atheist. He believes in the great Lord, and at the same time he is worried! What kind of belief is that? If I have firm faith that the Lord is there to take care of everything, that He has given me power, ability, and my work is only to serve Him, then I have no agitation. Then I am indeed on the path of devotion.

The third way to attain peace of mind is through the path of *dharma* (righteousness). When something that has to be done is not done, or we do something that we should not be doing, there is agitation. If a child does not do his homework, he will be fearful of the teacher's wrath. This applies to us also. If something is left unfinished, we will always be agitated by the thought of it. Only when we do the work will we be at peace. Therefore, if one performs all of one's obligatory duties and stays away from prohibited actions, then one is never agitated. For one who follows the path of *dharma*, there is no fear.

If one can follow any one of the paths he will surely attain peace. If one does not have an inquiring, analyzing intellect, it is all right. He can have simple faith; the Lord will take care of everything. Without faith, even a householder's life becomes miserable. If partners have distrust between them, there will be disharmony. Where there is faith there is peace.

Peace is the true nature of the mind, not agitation. That is why when agitation is there, we want to go back to a state of peace. We ourselves are creating the causes for agitation, which are desires, cravings, I-ness, my-ness, lack of faith, and non-performance of our duties. If we put forth effort to remove these causal factors of agitation, we will have true peace of mind.

XI

Peace of Mind: A Birthright
by J.P. Vaswani

Like love, peace is to be felt. I may tell you what peace is in many words, but you will not understand those words until you yourself have felt peace in the heart within.

There is truly one way of achieving peace of mind. And that is the way of Self-realization. Once you realize yourself, there is no more tension, no more stress. You abide in a state of tranquility and peace. You may not be able to achieve it overnight. It is a process through which you have to move.

Therefore, one very easy way of attaining peace of mind is to sit in silence everyday for 10 to 15 minutes and explain to yourself this one thing — that whatever happens, happens according to the will of God.

Why is it that we lose our peace of mind? Because our wishes, our desires are crossed. I want a particular thing to be done in a particular manner, it has happened in an opposite manner, my peace is disturbed.

A girl met me this afternoon. She said, "I don't want my child to cry but the child keeps on crying all the time. That disturbs my peace." Then I asked her, "Were you a child at any time?" She said, "Of course, I was a child only 20 years ago." I asked, "Did you ever cry?" "Of course I cried," came the reply. Then I asked, "Why don't you permit your child to cry? You cried and you don't permit your child to cry!"

We must understand, that whatever happens, happens according to the Will of God. This, which has happened contrary to my wishes, contrary to my desires, has happened according to God's Will. There must be some good in it for me.

Accept His Will

Explain this to your mind everyday, "O mind, why is it that you lose your peace? You lose your peace, because your wishes are not fulfilled. But above your wishes is the Will of God. Accept His Will and you will never lose your peace."

You will get peace of mind if you give your own "piece" to others. The great saint, Tulsidas says:

*Tulasī is saṁsāra meṁ kara līje do kāma,
dene ko ṭukḍā bhalā, lene ko Hari nāma.*

He says, keep on giving. When you have learnt to give, you have learnt to live all right. Then peace automatically wakes up in the heart within. It is only because we are so selfish that our peace is disturbed. Peace is our original nature. We are built of peace.

What is it that has disturbed our peace? Sordid selfishness. We have to overcome this selfishness, only then can we return to our original state. Each one of us is *sat-cit-ānanda*. *Ānanda* is the peace that can never be disturbed. *Ānanda* is the joy, the bliss that no ending knows. We have only to get back to our original state.

Ānandam is your birthright as children of God. Each one of you is a son or a daughter of God. And God is the source of *Ānanda*. He is an unending source of bliss. The moment I realize that I am a child of God, nothing is going to affect me. In order to live a life of bliss, all we have to do is to transcend the phenomenal, transcend what is happening around us.

You must have seen on several occasions when your mind is terribly disturbed and you go and do a little painting, you find that you have become peaceful suddenly. Why? Because you forgot yourself in this creative work. Likewise, when we move out of ourselves and give joy to those who are in need of joy, we forget ourselves.

All we need to do is to forget ourselves and peace will be ours. When we forget this outer self, we draw closer to the real, the inner Self, which is peace.

God loves each one of us with a love that is immeasurable. He has given us the most perfect machine — the human body — and the most perfect computer — the human brain. Let us not forget that every breath is valuable and must be spend in worthwhile pursuits. Let us set aside a portion of our daily food for a hungry one — a man, a bird, an animal. Let us speak the truth, kindly and softly and do all we can, to help as many as we can, to lift the load on the rough road of life. That is the way to peace.

XII

Making Peace with Yourself

by John Dear

A few years before his death in 1999, the great Latin American advocate for the poor, Brazil's Archbishop Dom Holder Camara was speaking at a crowded church in Berkeley California. He was asked, "After facing death squads, would-be assassins, corporations oppressing the poor, violent government opposition, and even hostile forces within our own church, who is your most difficult opponent?"

Without saying a word, Dom Helder pointed his hand into the air, then slowly arched it around, until it turned on himself, his index finger pointing to his heart. "I am my own worst enemy," he said, "my most difficult adversary. Here I have the greatest struggle for peace."

Likewise, Mahatma Gandhi was once asked about his greatest enemy. He spoke of the British and his struggle against imperialism. Then he reflected on his own people and his struggles against untouchability, bigotry and violence in India. Finally he spoke of himself, and his own inner violence, selfishness, and imperfection. The last, he confessed, was his greatest opponent. "There I have very little say."

If we want to make peace with others, we first need to be at peace with ourselves. But this can sometimes be as difficult as making peace in the bloodiest of the world's war zones.

Those who knew Dom Helder Camara and Mahatma Gandhi testify that they radiated a profound personal peace. But such

MAKING PEACE WITH YOURSELF

peace came at a great price: a lifelong inner struggle. They knew that to practice peace and nonviolence, you have to look within.

Peace begins within each of us. It is a process of repeatedly showing mercy to ourselves, forgiving ourselves, befriending ourselves, accepting ourselves, and loving ourselves. As we learn to appreciate ourselves and accept God's gift of peace, we begin to radiate peace and love to others.

This lifelong journey toward inner peace requires regular self-examination and an ongoing process of making peace with ourselves. It means constantly examining the roots of violence within us, weeding out those roots, diffusing the violence that we aim at ourselves and others, and choosing to live in peace. It means treating ourselves with compassion and kindness. As we practice mercy toward ourselves, we begin to enjoy life more and more and celebrate it as adventure in peace. We turn again and again to the God who created us and offer sincere thanks. By persistently refraining from violence and hatred and opening up to that spirit of peace and mercy, we live life to the fullest, and help make the world better for others.

The Daily Challenge

But this process of making peace with ourselves can be one of the most difficult challenges we face. Each one of us wrestles with our own demons. The daily challenge is to befriend those demons, embrace our true selves, make friends with ourselves, disarm our hearts, and accept in peace who we are. The deeper we go into our true identities, the more we will realize that each one of us is a unique yet beloved child of the God of peace. In that truth, we find the strength to live in peace.

For some, this inner struggle is just too difficult. Many prefer to endure their inner wars, believing that they cannot change, that inner peace is not realizable, that life is just too hard. Others succumb to violence and despair. I well remember my friend Mitch Snyder, the leading advocate for the homeless. For nearly twenty years, Mitch spoke out against poverty, organized demonstrations for housing, fasted for social change, and was arrested for civil disobedience on behalf of justice for the poor. He was director of the largest homeless shelter in the U.S., a facility with over one thousand beds just three blocks from the U.S. Capitol in Washington, D.C. In the mid-1980s, while I was managing a small church shelter for the homeless in Washington, D. C., I often visited with Mitch and discussed the plight of the homeless and our campaign to secure decent, affordable housing for them.

Mitch gave his life for the forgotten and the poor, but became consumed by his anger against the system that oppresses the poor into homelessness. He advocated nonviolence, but suffered many personal demons, which eventually got the best of him. For years, Mitch fought to gain local legislation guaranteeing the right of every person to shelter. Finally, in 1990, his effort was defeated. At the same time, a personal relationship broke down. On July 3, 1990, he gave in to despair, and killed himself. His suicide shocked and saddened us all.

Even though Mitch espoused justice and nonviolence eloquently on behalf of the most disenfranchised people in the nation, he could not maintain that same spirit of nonviolence toward himself, and the violence inside him literally destroyed him. His death challenged many of us who knew him to reexamine our own commitments and the violence within us, and to cultivate peace within, even as we continue to work actively for peace and justice.

"Love your neighbors as you love yourselves," Jesus tells us. As we love and accept ourselves, we will find strength to love others, and to love God, who loved us first. As we make peace with ourselves, we can learn to make peace with others. Such true self-love is not selfishness, egotism, or narcissism, but wholeness, even holiness. First, we humbly accept our brokenness, our weakness, our limitations, our frailty and vulnerability, and our dependence on God. We accept our failures and forgive ourselves for our mistakes. Then, we accept the living God who dwells within us, and allow God's peace to make Her home within us. Making peace with ourselves is like building an inner house of peace and welcoming the God of peace to dwell there forever.

"While you are proclaiming peace with your lips." St. Francis of Assisi advised, "be careful to have it even more fully in your heart." St. Francis put down his sword, took up the life of peace, found his heart disarmed, and started serving the poor. Everywhere he went, he proclaimed the good news of peace and people would flock to hear him, just to be in his presence, because he radiated peace.

Cultivating Inner Peace

But inner peace does not mean we float around in blissful tranquility, talking to the birds, untouched by everyday mishaps, personal tragedies, or world events. In fact, true inner peace pushes us into the thick of the world's problems, where we rub elbows with all kinds of people and confront their greatest terrors, as St. Francis did. From the hustle and bustle of a crowded subway to the death of a loved one to turmoil at the workplace to the threat of nuclear destruction, life presents daily challenges to our inner resolve. But it is possible to cultivate and pursue inner peace no matter what obstacles come our way. Through the grace of God, all our frustrations, turmoil, and tragedies can be transformed.

The inner life of peace means acting from a deep conviction about who we are, that each one of us is a beloved child of God, a human being called to love and serve other human beings. Living from this conviction does not mean we ignore our emotions — quite the contrary. In fact, as we go forward into the world, to places like death row, soup kitchens, or war zones, we touch the pain of the world and feel the full range of human emotions, with sorrow and anger, as we experience the pain of human tragedy and injustice.

In 1985, while living in a refugee camp in El Salvador's war zone, I felt terrible sorrow, grief, and outrage as I witnessed the death and destruction around me, but I also felt a great inner peace because I clung to my faith in the God of peace, who seemed palpably present in the suffering people around me. Deep down, I rested in God's peace and even felt joy while I endured and resisted the horror of war with the refugees around me.

Our inner peace is not self-satisfied. We cannot idly pursue inner tranquility while wars, bombings, executions, greed, and violence continue unchallenged. If we do not address the violence in the world, our inner peace is an empty illusion. Likewise, we cannot seek peace publicly and expect to help disarm the world while our hearts are filled with violence, judgment, and rage. Our work for peace cannot bear fruit if it is rooted in violence.

"One of the reasons why so many people have developed strong reservations about the peace movement is precisely that they do not see the peace they seek in the peacemakers themselves," the spiritual writer Henri Nouwen once observed. "Often what they see are fearful and angry people trying to convince others of the urgency of their protest. The tragedy is that peacemakers often reveal more of the demons they are fighting than of the peace they want to bring about."[1]

The roots of war, violence, injustice, and the threat of global annihilation lie within each one of us. Unless we recognize our complicity in global violence, we can never accept God's gift of peace. If however, we recognize, acknowledge and confess the violence within us, we allow God to begin the process of our disarmament, first in our own war-torn hearts, and then in the world itself.

God's Peace Within Us

As we pursue this inner journey and disarm our hearts, heal our internal divisions, seek inner reconciliation, and make peace

MAKING PEACE WITH YOURSELF

with the God within, we can speak about disarmament, reconciliation, and peace with greater authenticity and integrity. Like Dom Helder Camara, Mahatma Gandhi, St. Francis, and Mother Teresa, we begin to embody our message, because our message is rooted in our very being, in the God of peace who lives in us. Our peace will spread out around us, even throughout the world, because it will be God's own peace springing forth.

Thomas Merton wrote that Gandhi's nonviolence "sprang from an inner realization of spiritual unity in himself. The whole Gandhian concept of nonviolent action and *satyāgraha* [firm in truth] is incomprehensible if it is thought to be a means of achieving unity rather than as the fruit of inner unity already achieved."[2] In other words, Gandhi had plumbed the depths of peace within himself. He renounced inner violence, advocated public nonviolence, and so, radiated peace to a world at war.

"Nonviolence is not a garment to be put on and off at will," Gandhi wrote. "Its seat is in the heart, and it must be an inseparable part of our very being. Nonviolence is a matter of the heart. It implies as complete self-purification as is humanly possible."[3]

Pursuing peace at every level of life — beginning within our own hearts and souls, and reaching out toward every human being alive on the planet — is the greatest and most fulfilling challenge one can undertake with one's life. But making peace in a world at war is an act greater than any of us. It is a spiritual journey that begins in the heart and takes us on a road not of our own choosing. But because it is a spiritual journey, a course charted by the God of peace, it is filled with the simplest but greatest of blessings.

As we make peace with ourselves, and welcome the God of peace who lives within us, we will learn to make peace with those around us and with others throughout the world. Over time, we will become true instruments of God's own peace and help make the world a better, more just place for all. The challenge is to do both: To pursue peace within and to pursue peace with the whole human race.

JOHN DEAR

That journey, though difficult, promises a happy ending. We will be ready to meet the God of peace face to face when our time comes because we will have spent our lives welcoming God here and now in our hearts. We will look back and see that our lives have been a step-by-step pilgrimage from peace to peace until that great day when we enter God's own house of peace.

FOOTNOTES:

1. John Dear, editor, *The Road to Peace: Writings on Peace* by Henri Nouwen. Maryknoll: Orbis Books, 1997, p.41
2. Thomas Merton, editor, *Gandhi on Nonviolence*. New York: New Directions, 1964, p. 6
3. Merton p. 24; and, Eknath Easwaran, *Gandhi the Man*. Tomales, Calif.: Nilgiri Press, 1997, p. 116

XIII

Peacefully Remaining

by Sogyal Rinpoche

Meditation is bringing the mind back home, and this is first achieved through the practice of mindfulness. Once an old woman came to Buddha and asked him how to meditate. He told her to remain aware of every movement of her hands as she drew the water from the well, knowing that if she did, she would soon find herself in that state of alert and spacious calm that is meditation.

The practice of mindfulness, of bringing the scattered mind home, and so of bringing the different aspects of our being into focus, is called "Peacefully Remaining" or "Calm Abiding." "Peacefully Remaining" accomplishes three things. First, all the fragmented aspects of ourselves, which have been at war, settle and dissolve and become friends. In that settling we begin to understand ourselves more, and sometimes even have glimpses of the radiance of our fundamental nature.

Second, the practice of mindfulness defuses our negativity, aggression, and turbulent emotions, which may have been gathering power over many lifetimes. Rather than suppressing emotions or indulging in them, here it is important to view them, and your thoughts, and whatever arises with an acceptance and generosity that are as open and spacious as possible. Tibetan masters say that this wise generosity has the flavor of boundless space, so warm and cozy that you feel enveloped and protected by it, as if by a blanket of sunlight.

Gradually as you remain open and mindful, and use one of the techniques that I will explain later to focus your mind more and more, your negativity will slowly be defused; you begin to feel well in your being, or as the French say, *être bien dans sa peau* (well in your own skin). From this come release and a profound ease. I think of this practice as the most effective form of therapy and self-healing.

Third, this practice unveils and reveals your essential Good Heart, because it dissolves and removes the unkindness or the harm in you. Only when we have removed the harm in ourselves do we become truly useful to others. Through the practice, then, by slowly removing the unkindness and harm from ourselves, we allow our true Good Heart, the fundamental goodness and kindness that are our real nature, to shine out and become the warm climate in which our true being flowers.

You will see now why I call meditation the true practice of peace, the true practice of non-aggression and nonviolence, and the real and greatest disarmament.

Natural Great Peace

When I teach meditation, I often begin by saying: "Bring your mind home. And release. And relax."

The whole meditation practice can be essentialized into these three crucial points: Bring your mind home, and release, and relax. Each phrase contains meanings that resonate on many levels.

To bring your mind home means to bring the mind into the state of Calm Abiding through the practice of mindfulness. In its deepest sense, to bring your mind home is to turn your mind inward and to rest in the nature of mind. This itself is the highest meditation.

To release means to release mind from its prison of grasping, since you recognize that all pain and fear and distress arise from the craving of the grasping mind. On a deeper level, the realization and confidence that arise from your growing understanding of the nature of mind inspire the profound and natural generosity that enables you to release all grasping from your heart, letting it free itself, to melt away in the inspiration of meditation.

Finally, *to relax* means to be spacious and to relax the mind of its tensions. More deeply, you relax into the true nature of your mind, the state of *Rigpa*. The Tibetan words that evoke this process suggest the sense of "relaxing *upon* the *Rigpa*." It is like pouring a handful of sand onto a flat surface; each grain settles of its own accord. This is how you relax into your true nature, letting all thoughts and emotions naturally subside and dissolve into the state of the nature of mind.

When I meditate, I am always inspired by this poem by Nyoshul Khenpo:

> Rest in natural great peace
> This exhausted mind
> Beaten helpless by karma and neurotic thought.
> Like the relentless fury of the pounding waves
> In the infinite ocean of *saṁsāra*.

Rest in natural great peace. Above all, be at ease, be as natural and spacious as possible. Slip quietly out of the noose of your habitual anxious self, release all grasping, and relax into your true nature. Think of your ordinary, emotional, thought-ridden self as a block of ice or a slab of butter left out in the sun. If you are feeling hard and cold, let this aggression melt away in the sunlight of your meditation. Let peace work on you and enable you to gather your scattered mind into the mindfulness of Calm Abiding, and awaken in you the awareness and insight of Clear Seeing. And you will find all your negativity disarmed, your aggression dissolved, and your confusion evaporating slowly, like mist into the vast and stainless sky of your absolute nature[1].

Quietly sitting, body still, speech silent, mind at peace, let thoughts and emotions, whatever rises, come and go, without clinging to anything

What does this state feel like? Dudjom Rinpoche used to say imagine a man who comes home after a long, hard day's work in the fields, and sinks into his favorite chair in front of the fire. He has been working all day and he knows that he has achieved what he wanted to achieve; there is nothing more to worry about, nothing left unaccomplished, and he can let go completely of all his cares and concerns, content simply to be.

So when you meditate, it is essential to create the right inner environment of the mind. All effort and struggle come from not being spacious, and so creating that right environment is vital for your meditation truly to happen. When humor and spaciousness are present, meditation arises effortlessly.

Sometimes when I meditate, I don't use any particular method. I just allow my mind to rest, and find, especially when I am inspired that I can bring my mind home and relax very quickly. I sit quietly and rest in the nature of mind; I don't question or doubt whether I am in the "correct" state or not. There is no effort, only rich understanding, wakefulness, and unshakable certainty. When I am in the nature of mind, the ordinary mind is no longer there. There is no need to sustain or confirm a sense of being: I simply am. A fundamental trust is present. There is nothing in particular to do.

FOOTNOTE:

[1] "Calm Abiding" and "Clear Seeing" are the two central practices of Buddhist meditation, called in Sanskrit *Samatā* and *Vipaścanā*, and in Tibetan *Shyiné* and *Lhaktong*.

Part Four

Peacemakers

*Peace is not a relationship of nations.
It is a condition of mind brought about by a serenity of soul.
Lasting peace can come only to peaceful people.*

Jawaharlal Nehru

No one, not at any rate, he who has perfected himself, can be at ease when the world cries for help. The well-being of others becomes his deepest concern. He loves his fellows with a tenderness and depth unknown to others. He can no more help loving humanity than a sunflower can help pointing to the sun. To be saved is not to enter a region of blissful ease and unending rest.

The saved one becomes an elemental force of nature, a dynamo of spirit, working at a stupendously high velocity. The renunciation he has practiced does not require him to flee from the world of works but only to slay the ego sense. Eternal life is here and now. It is the life of the eternal part of us, of the light within us, of intelligence and love, whose objects are incorruptible.

S. Radhakrishnan

XIV

The Words of Peace

Edited by Irwin Abrams

[The Nobel Peace Prize Laureates of The Twentieth Century, selections from their Acceptance Speeches. The date after the name denotes year of the prize.]

Norman Angell (1933)

Man's greatest advances these last few generations have been made by the application of human intelligence to the management of matter. Now we are confronted by a more difficult problem, the application of intelligence to the management of human relations. Unless we can advance in that field also, the very instruments that man's intelligence has created may be the instruments of his destruction.

The obstacles to peace are not obstacles in matter, in inanimate nature, in the mountains, which we pierce, in the seas across which we fly. The obstacles to peace are in the minds and hearts of men.

In the study of matter we can be honest, impartial, true. That is why we succeed in dealing with it. But about the things we care for — which are ourselves, our desires and lusts, our patriotism and hates — we find a harder test of thinking straight and truly. Yet there is the greater need. Only by intellectual rectitude in that field shall we be saved. There is no refuge but in truth, in human intelligence, in the unconquerable mind of man.

Norman Angell 1872-1967, British author of the noted peace book The Great Illusion, *who served the cause for many years as a very influential publicist and lecturer.*

THE WORDS OF PEACE

Ralph J. Bunche (1950)

Peace is no mere matter of men fighting or not fighting. Peace, to have meaning for many who have known only suffering in both peace and war, must be translated into bread or rice, shelter, health, and education, as well as freedom and human dignity — a steadily better life. If peace is to be secure, long-suffering and long-starved, forgotten peoples of the world, the underprivileged and the undernourished, must begin to realize without delay the promise of a new day and a new life.

Ralph J. Bunche (1904-1971), American social scientist who served as a state Department official and then as a top UN administrator. As UN mediator, he negotiated the ending of the Arab-Jewish hostilities over Palestine in 1949.

Martin Luther King, Jr. (1964)

All that I have said boils down to the point of affirming that mankind's survival is dependent upon man's ability to solve the problems of racial injustice, poverty, and war; the solution of these problems is in turn dependent upon man's squaring his moral progress with his scientific progress, and learning the practical art of living in harmony....

So we must fix our vision not merely on the negative expulsion of war, but upon the positive affirmation of peace. We must see that peace represents a sweet music, a cosmic melody that is far superior to the discords of war. Somehow we must transform the dynamics of the world power struggle from the negative nuclear arms race, which no one can win to a positive contest to harness man's creative genius for the purpose of making peace and prosperity a reality for all of the nations of the world. In short, we must shift the arms race into a peace race. If we have the will and determination to mount such a peace offensive, we will unlock hitherto tightly sealed doors of hope and transform our imminent cosmic elegy into a psalm of creative fulfillment.

IRWIN ABRAMS

Martin Luther King (1929-1968), the leader of the nonviolent movement for civil rights in the U.S.A., Baptist minister who had undertaken advanced studies; his sermons and speeches are considered among the best examples of American oratory. The Chairman of the Norwegian Nobel committee declared: "He is the first person in the Western world to have shown us that a struggle can be waged without violence. He is the first to make the message of brotherly love a reality in the course of his struggle, and he has brought this message to all men, to all nations and races."

Poul Hartling (1981)

"Peace is more than just absence of war. It is rather a state in which no people of any country, in fact no group of people of any kind live in fear or in need...." Today, more than ten million refugees live in fear or in need. On our road towards a better future for mankind we certainly cannot ignore the tragic presence of those millions for whom peace does not exist. Whenever we solve one single problem we have contributed to peace for the individual. Whenever we bring peace to the individual we are making our world a slightly better place in which to live.
Poul Hartling, representing the Office of the United Nations High Commissioner for refugees, and quoting from the 1954 speech of Dr. G. Jan van Heuven Goedhart.

The Dalai Lama (1989)

Peace starts within each one of us. When we have inner peace, we can be at peace with those around us. When our community is in a state of peace, it can share that peace with neighboring communities, and so on. When we feel love and kindness towards others, it not only makes others feel loved and cared for, but it helps us also to develop inner happiness and peace. ...
I feel honored, humbled and deeply moved that you should

give this important prize to a simple monk from Tibet. I am no one special. But I believe the prize is a recognition of the true value of altruism, love, compassion and nonviolence which I try to practice, in accordance with the teachings of the Buddha and the great sages of India and Tibet. ...

As a Buddhist monk, my concern extends to all members of the human family and, indeed, to all sentient beings who suffer. I believe all suffering is caused by ignorance. People inflict pain on others in the selfish pursuit of their happiness or satisfaction. Yet true happiness comes from a sense of inner peace and contentment, which in turn must be achieved through the cultivation of altruism, of love and compassion, and elimination of ignorance, selfishness, and greed.

Dalai Lama XIV of Tibet, Tenzin Gyatso (1935-) Enthroned in 1940 as the spiritual and temporal ruler of Tibet, he went into exile in India in 1959, after the Chinese, who regard Tibet as part of China, sent in their army to establish control. Since then he has worked untiringly from abroad to liberate his people. He was given the prize for championing of human rights by the means of nonviolence, for his Buddhist message of love and compassion, and for his efforts to awaken concern for the environment.

Carlos Filipe Ximenes Belo (1996)

Let it be stated clearly that to make peace a reality, we must be flexible as well as wise. We must truly recognize our own faults and move to change ourselves in the interest of making peace. I am no exception to this rule! Let us banish anger and hostility, vengeance and other dark emotions, and transform ourselves into humble instruments of peace. People in East Timor are not uncompromising. They are not unwilling to forgive and overcome their bitterness. On the contrary, they yearn for peace, peace within their community and peace in their region. They wish to build bridges with their Indonesian brothers and sisters, to find ways of creating harmony and tolerance.

IRWIN ABRAMS

Carlos Filipe Ximenes Belo (1946-). Born on the tropical island of Timor, in 1988 he was consecrated as bishop. He was a vocal advocate for the human rights of the people of East Timor. His work led to several proclamations issued by the United Nations that criticized Indonesia and embarrassed its leaders. He was awarded the Nobel Peace prize for his dedicated defense of the human rights to the East Timorese.

Nathan Soderblom (1930)

If peace is to become a reality on our earth, it must be founded in the hearts of the people. To whom should this task belong if not to the church, which calls itself the Prince of Peace and has as its watchword what is also a divine promise: Glory to God in the highest and peace on earth. The human heart is fickle, and therefore peace must, according to the words of the prophets, be safeguarded by law and order, by a supranational judicial system which has the power to assert itself against nations endangering peace and which, without bias or compromise holds justice to be the highest law. Nevertheless, any such legal system, however wise and strong, remains a mere shell if not supported by mankind's concern for peace and liberty.

Nathan Soderblom (1866-1931) As Archbishop of Uppsala and the top prelate of Sweden, he took world leadership in working for peace through the ecumenical movement.

John Hume (1998)

All conflict is about difference; whether the difference is race, religion or nationality, the European visionaries decided that difference is not a threat, difference is natural. Difference is of the essence of humanity. Difference is an accident of birth and it should therefore never be the source of hatred or conflict. The answer to difference is to respect it. Therein lies a most fundamental principle of peace; respect for diversity.

THE WORDS OF PEACE

John Hume (1937-) an enduring figure on Northern Ireland's political stage, he spent decades working toward a resolution of the province's sectarian conflict. As leader of the Social Democratic and Labour Party (SDLP), the main moderate nationalist party of Northern Ireland's Catholic minority, he steadfastly denounced the violent tactics of the paramilitary Irish Republican Army (IRA) and pursued closer ties with the overwhelmingly Catholic Republic of Ireland through peaceful means only. His efforts to bring Sinn Fein, a Catholic party with ties to the IRA, into peace negotiations made him instrumental in forging a landmark all-party accord in 1998.

Mother Teresa (1979)

And with this prize that I have received as a Prize of Peace, I am going to try to make the home for many people who have no home. Because I believe that love begins at home, and if we can create a home for the poor I think that more and more love will spread. And we will be able through this understanding love to bring peace, be the good news to the poor. The poor in our own family first, in our country and in the world. To be able to do this, our Sisters, our lives have to be woven with prayer. They have to be woven with Christ to be able to understand, to be able to share. Because to be woven with Christ is to be able to understand, to be able to share. Because today there is so much suffering.... When I pick up a person from the street, hungry, I give him a plate of rice, a piece of bread, I have satisfied. I have removed that hunger. But a person who is shut out, who feels unwanted, unloved, terrified, the person who has been thrown out from society — that poverty is so full of hurt and so unbearable, and I find that very difficult. ... And so let us always meet each other with a smile, for the smile is the beginning of love, and once we begin to love each other naturally we want to do something.

Mother Teresa (1910-1999) known as the "Saint of Calcutta" for her works of mercy for the poor in its slums. Born to an Alba-

nian family in what is now Yugoslav Macedonia, she joined a Catholic teaching order to serve in its missionary school in Calcutta, but overwhelmed by the poverty and misery she found there, she heeded the call to leave the convent and to help the poor while living among them. As she cared for the hungry, the sick, and the dying, others joined her, and she founded a new order, the Missionaries of Charity, whose good works have reached far beyond India to centers of need all over the world.

Frederik W. de Klerk (1993)

The greatest peace, I believe, is the peace which we derive from our faith in God Almighty; from certainty about our relationship with our Creator. Crises might beset us, battles might rage about us — but if we have faith and the certainty it brings, we will enjoy peace — the peace that surpasses all understanding.

Frederik W. de Klerk (1936-) Son of a leading politician of South Africa, he graduated in law and became a prominent member of the ruling National Party. After holding a number of ministerial posts, in 1989 he became the leader of the party and then state president. In 1990 he freed Nelson Mandela from prison, and courageously reversing the policies of his party, dismantled apartheid and worked with Mandela to prepare the way for free non-racist elections. For their cooperation in peacefully ending the racial conflict and laying the foundation for a new democratic country, he received the prize. As a result of the elections, de Klerk became a vice-president of South Africa. He later withdrew from political life.

Nelson Mandela (1993)

We live with the hope that as she battles to remake herself, South Africa will be like a microcosm of the new world that is striving to be born. This must be a world of democracy and respect for human rights, a world freed from the horrors of poverty, hunger, deprivation and ignorance, relieved of the threat and the scourge of civil wars and external aggression and unburdened of the great tragedy of millions forced to become refugees.

The processes in which South Africa and Southern Africa as a whole are engaged, beckon and urge us all that we take this tide at the flood and make of this region a living example of what all people of conscience would like the world to be.

Nelson Mandela was president of the African National Congress (ANC) when he shared the Nobel Peace prize with President Frederick W. de Klerk of the Republic of South Africa. In 1990 de Klerk had freed him from prison, where Mandela had been incarcerated for almost 28 years for his activities opposing apartheid and where he had become the most celebrated prisoner of the time and the symbol of the struggle in South Africa for racial justice. He emerged from prison to assume the leadership of the ABD and, unembittered and in the spirit of reconciliation, to cooperate with de Klerk to end apartheid and to arrange for free, all-race elections. For thus ending the conflict peacefully, the two were granted the prize. The elections, held in 1994, resulted in Mandela's replacing de Klerk as state president. He served until 1999.

XV

Nelson Mandela and the Rainbow of Culture

by Anders Hallengren

[The following article is excerpted from a comprehensive biography.]

Equality and Pluralism

After 27 years in prison, Nelson Mandela negotiated the dismantling of the apartheid regime in South Africa, settled an agreement on universal suffrage and democratic elections, and became the first black president of the country in 1994. When he entered into office, he was aware of the universal importance of this success, but he was also humbled by the focus on his person as a symbol of international and historical dimensions. After all, during the years 1952-1990, he had made only three public appearances, and numerous people of different nations had contributed to the cause. Indeed, Africa had been liberated from colonialism during his prison years. The truth of the ancient Bantu adage *umuntu ngumuntu ngabantu* (we are people through other people) often came to his mind. And he saw, perhaps clearer than most of his contemporaries, the inevitability of "mutual interdependence" in the human condition, that "the common ground is greater and more enduring than the differences that divide." The background of the development of this vision is remarkable and diverse. From his African heritage, from his country's turbulent history, from his own formal education in "colonial" schools, and from his vicissitudes in the confines of Robben Island, Mandela emerged a man with a singular vision.

The Development of "Color-blindness"

Starting his fight for liberation of the blacks as an aggressive young African pugilist and nationalist in the early 1940's, Mandela had not always deemed that democratic progress must rest on equality, pluralism, and multi-ethnicity. What made him later stand out from other South African leaders, and made him finally emerge victorious, was precisely his vision of a state that belongs equally to all its different peoples, nations, and tribes, whether Afrikaan, English, or Zulu. Being himself a leader belonging to the Xhosa-speaking people, he eventually transcended the idea of national liberty, and he attracted Indians, Jews, and other segments of the multicolored population to the cause. Countering the racist suppression of the blacks, he avoided, unlike many other revolutionaries of the continent, acceding to a basically or exclusively black or tribal liberation movement.

This vision, sometimes referred to as "color-blindness," was partly inspired by Marxists, drawing on European ideologies and influenced from abroad. They were internationalists, not nationalists, and fought for a class, not for a race. The South African Communist Party, originally founded in 1920, and the kernel of which was a small group of Jewish immigrants and English nonconformists, was to influence the African National Congress (ANC) in such a direction, without ever succeeding in turning Nelson Mandela, Oliver Tambo, and other leaders into members of their party. This influence was theoretical and ideological, based on reading, hearsay, and revolutionary tradition. Through the years, it also became increasingly economic, in terms of financial support from parts of the communist, the socialist, and the social-democratic world, including Sweden,

Norway, and India as well as the USSR. Mandela's party, the ANC, was completely pragmatic in its views of material means, however. It accepted succour and aid wherever it came from, whether from Libya (as it happens, one of Mandela's grandchildren was baptized "Gadaffi"), Iraq, diamond investors, or multinational corporations, sticking to its cause and never deviating from its course. The Sotho maxim "many rills make a big river" often was in Mandela's mind. As a matter of fact, and quite contrary to contemporary European and American views, Nelson Mandela and the ANC remained ideologically independent while their financial dependence grew. Nevertheless, as a result of this focus and political imbalance, the ANC became a pawn in great-power politics, which delayed Mandela's release and peaceful reform in South Africa until the winding-up of the Eastern bloc in 1989-90.

The Legacy of Mahatma Gandhi and Pandit Nehru

Another source of transnational perspectives and ideas of coexistence in harmony was the likewise oppressed Indian population of South Africa, many of whom traced their origin from the indentured laborers shipped to local sugar cane fields by the British colonial authorities. The confidence and faith of contemporary Indian freedom fighters rested upon the belief in the *Satyagraha* (truth-power) preached and put into effect by Mahatma Gandhi, a vision that had freed India in 1947. The vision of Gandhi was kept alive and thrived in South Africa, where Gandhi himself had lived and worked for many years (1893-1914). Nelson Mandela's early encounters with these more peaceful Hindu, as well as Moslem, activists and their ideologies of emancipation seriously complicated his view of African liberation, and a close bond between the ANC and South Africa's Indian population developed over time. This personal encounter with other people's liberation movements in South Africa, eventually — almost of necessity, as it were — made the ANC leadership turn multicultural and multi-religious, bound together by a common goal and based on that "common ground" Mandela often refers to. ...

M.K. Gandhi, Attorney in South Africa, was in a deep sense succeeded by Nelson Mandela, Johannesburg Attorney. Or, as Nelson Mandela said in September 1992, when he had been released from prison and democratic reform was on the agenda:

> Gandhiji was a South African and his memory deserves to be cherished now and in post-apartheid South Africa. We must never lose sight of the fact that the Gandhian philosophy may be a key to human survival in the twenty-first century.

Manilal Gandhi, the son of Mahatma, remained in his father's house in Natal, South Africa, and the Indian reform movement encouraged the chaotic but awakening civil disobedience campaigns shaking large parts of South Africa in the early 1950's, in particular the Defiance Campaign of 1952, where the internal passport laws and other apartheid measures were challenged. These originally Indian-inspired peaceful resistance initiatives were met by violence, and the movements gradually turned underground, where they eventually grew. Finally the ANC reacted by building a military command, the *Umkhonto we Sizwe* (Spear of the Nation), preparing itself for guerrilla war. Contrary to Gandhi, and unlike the ANC leader Albert Lutuli, who received the Nobel Peace Prize in 1960, or Archbishop Desmund Tutu, Peace Prize Laureate of 1984, Nelson Mandela long felt forced to advocate unavoidable revolutionary violence, considering it as a counter-violence or a justified uprising against iniquitous laws. Mandela eventually dressed himself in camouflage uniform and was in combat training abroad (in Ethiopia), as were many other revolutionaries. Banned by the South African regime from attending public gatherings from late 1952 on, he nevertheless had efficiently and ingeniously continued his work as an organizer through undercover actions, escaping the police in ever-changing disguises, one of the favorites being that of a chauffeur. The years before his final imprisonment in 1962, he was nicknamed "The Black Pimpernel."

Still, the Indian heritage of peaceful resistance was present in Mandela's mind, and one of his closest fellow-combatants and conspirators was the Indian Ahmed Kathrada, with whom he was to spend a quarter of a century in jail. Among Mandela's models and teachers, however, Jawaharlal Nehru — more militant than Gandhi and a politician of a practical turn — had become the prominent figure.

We should recall that his Indian friends evoked Mandela's interest in India at the time when that state was in the process of being liberated from British colonialism. Nehru, who in 1947 became the first Prime Minister of India, had for two decades urged the Indians in South Africa to join forces with the black Africans, and India was the first country to introduce sanctions against the apartheid regime. One of Mandela's most famous phrases and book titles, *No Easy Walk to Freedom,* was a quote from Nehru, whose hardships and determination he identified with. While in jail, Mandela was greatly encouraged by receiving the Indian Nehru Prize of 1979, and in his speech of thanks, in his absence read in New Delhi by the exiled Oliver Tambo, he emphasized his indebtedness to Nehru. Their fates were similar, too. When later on speaking of his release from prison, Nelson Mandela has said: "I was helped when preparing for my release by the biography of Pandit Nehru, who wrote of what happens when you leave jail. My daughter Zinzi says that she grew up without a father, who, when he returned, became a father of the nation."

XVI

Peace Pilgrim

by Ann and John Rush

[One of the most unusual modern witnesses of peace was a woman who called herself simply "Peace Pilgrim." For almost thirty years she walked across America imparting the message of peace to all who would listen.]

"I look forward to the time when my present-day garment returns to the dust from which it came, while my spirit goes on to a freer living," the woman known as Peace Pilgrim wrote. "Free of earth, as free as air, now you travel everywhere," a friend of hers wrote after her death.

Although she had no fear of death and even looked forward to it, Peace was a completely happy person in this world, thankful constantly for the beauty of the earth. "You will never be privileged to meet a happier person," wrote one minister.

Fellowship reported last September that Peace Pilgrim was killed in a head-on collision while being driven to a speaking engagement outside Knox, Indiana. She always insisted that we should rejoice with our loved ones who make the glorious transition. During the first year of her pilgrimage (1953), she was faced with death in a blinding snowstorm and called it the most beautiful experience of her life!

But like many of her other friends across the country we did not exactly receive the news of her death with rejoicing. Shock seemed to be the most frequently expressed feeling. Her life as a pilgrim was such a miracle, walking countless miles beyond twenty-five thousand because, she said, "I shall remain a wanderer until mankind has learned the way of peace, walking until I am given shelter, fasting until I am given food." Talking with people everywhere about the urgent need for peace, her words rang with true simplicity. As Robert Steele wrote in the Indian journal *Gandhi Marg*, "Peace Pilgrim speaks with astonishing authority and confidence: She reminds one of the spokesmen of God of biblical times." In another Indian journal the author wrote: "It's as though Gandhiji is speaking through her."

Twenty-four years ago this remarkable woman walked into our lives to begin the long friendship that was to have a profound influence on us both. We were living in the backwoods of British Columbia then, in a Quaker community; Peace was on her pilgrimage through Canada. When she spoke to Argenta Friends Meeting on the shores of Kootenay Lake, John said to her: "This is the same message the saints have given down through the ages." "I know there is nothing new in my message, except the practice of it," she replied.

Her message was always the same: "Overcome evil with good, falsehood with truth, and hatred with love." The universal truth she spoke, combined with her deep inner peace, made a profound impression on most of those who heard her. As the years went by she became so full of a contagious zest that her audiences responded more and more frequently with spontaneous laugher. She told stories of her pilgrimage and steps she took, not knowing where they were leading. They led to inner peace. "Inner peace comes through working for the good of all," she said. "Each one has a contribution to make, and will feel within what this contribution is."

Practicing the Simple Life

Inner peace had not come easily to this unusual woman. In her twenties she had a good job and a busy social life, but life eventually became meaningless. Out of a very deep seeking, she finally came to a complete willingness to give her life to service. That was thirty-three years ago. When the decision was made, a great peace came over her. With it, she knew that her life work would be for peace. Even afterward, she had "the great blessing of good health," she said. "I haven't had an ache or pain, a cold or headache since."

"I took daily walks, receptive and silent amid the beauties of nature, and wonderful insights would come to me which I then put into practice." Here is an example of one of those insights: "I came to feel the need for simplification of life. This was made easy for me because I felt I could no longer accept more than I need while others have less than they need." A fifteen-year preparation followed as she rid herself of "unnecessary possessions and meaningless activities" while doing volunteer work for FOR and other peace groups.

During this time, she experienced "a wonderful mountaintop experience."

> For the first time, I knew what inner peace was like. I felt a oneness with all my fellow human beings, with all creation. There is a feeling of always being surrounded by all of the good things like love and peace and joy. There is a feeling of endless energy; it just never runs out. You seem to be plugged into universal energy. It was only at this time that I felt called to begin my pilgrimage for peace in the world. One day, when I was taking a short walk through New England, I saw myself in a navy blue outfit with the words Peace Pilgrim on the front, walking across America.

In her first newsletter she wrote: "In undertaking this pilgrimage, I do not think of myself as an individual but rather as an embodiment of all human hearts that are pleading for peace."

Thus, Peace left her home twenty-eight years ago, without a penny or an organization backing her, with only the clothes she wore, a folding toothbrush, a pen, a comb, and copies of her message. She also left her name and earlier identity behind forever. From that time on, she never lacked what she needed to live. "Without ever asking for anything, I have been supplied with everything I need for my journey," she said. "You see how good people really are?"

After walking twenty-five thousand miles, she stopped counting in 1964; speaking became her first priority. This is the way she accounts for her ability to walk so far, beginning at forty-four years of age: "I walk not on the energy of youth, but the energy that comes with inner peace." Through all of the years during the McCarthy era, the Korean War, the Vietnam war, and since, Peace took her message to tens of thousands of people (probably well over a million; no one kept track), on city streets and dusty roads, in ghettos, suburbs, deserts, even truck stops (once, a stream of truckers kept her talking all night).

Through all of the years when most of us were becoming increasingly afraid to go out on city streets, she walked through slums, slept in bus stations, in trucks, and in the homes of strangers. She slept on the ground, covered with leaves, in cornfields, and in a box under a bridge. Strangers became friends inviting her into their homes and arranging speaking engagements, often a year or more in advance. In recent years she was able to sleep indoors about three-quarters of the time.

Peace Pilgrim has given us renewed hope in the future of this world, hope that many might gain enough inner peace to make world peace possible. She has strengthened our faith in the realm of the spiritual world and given us a concrete example of something we never dreamed possible: a person filled with inner peace and boundless energy that grew instead of diminishing with age. She has given us hope of finding that same Universal Energy because she insists it is there for all of us.

"If I can find it, you can, too," she would say. The greatest inspiration of all is that her life and her words were one. She was her message.

XVII

Gandhi and the Ancient Wisdom of Nonviolence

by *Mairead Corrigan Maguire*

[In 1977 Mairead Maguire received the Nobel Peace Prize, along with Betty Williams, for their efforts for peace in Northern Ireland. In the following article Mrs. Maguire addresses the Gandhian movement in India on the fiftieth anniversary of Gandhi's assassination]

Gandhi realized that the spirit of nonviolence begins within us and moves out from there. The life of active nonviolence is the fruit of an inner peace and spiritual unity already realized in us, and not the other way around. I have come to believe, with Gandhi, that through our own personal, inner conversion, our own inner peace, we are sensitized to care for God, ourselves, each other, for the poor, and for our world. Then we can become true servants of peace in the world. Herein lies the power of nonviolence. As our hearts are disarmed by God of our inner violence, they become God's instruments for the disarmament of the world. Without this inner conversion, we run the risk of becoming embittered, disillusioned, despairing, or simply burnt out, especially when our work for peace and justice appears to produce little or no result, or seems trifling in comparison with the injustice we see all around us. With this conversion we learn to let go of "all desires" — including the destructive desire to see results.

For many people, this ancient wisdom of the heart, the wisdom of nonviolence, may seem too religious and too idealistic in today's hardheaded world of politics and science. But I believe with Gandhi that we need to take an imaginative leap forward toward a fresh and generous idealism for the sake of all humanity. We need to renew this ancient wisdom of nonviolence, to strive for a disarmed world, and to create new nonviolence cultures.

As we enter the third millennium, we need to apply the wisdom of nonviolence to politics, economics, and science. For many, particularly in the West, increased materialism and unprecedented consumerism has not led to inner peace or happiness. Although technology has given us many benefits, it has not helped us distinguish between what enhances life and humanity and what destroys life and humanity. The time has come to return to the ancient wisdom.

When we examine where we are today, given the politics and technology of violence, we can only conclude that we live in an insane world.

Is it not insanity to go on producing nuclear and conventional weapons that if used can destroy millions of people, if not the whole planet?

Is it not insanity to spend billions of the people's money to produce and maintain these weapons of mass destruction, while millions of children die of disease and starvation each year? When (according to the UN) sixty thousand children die every day of starvation, even though the world's governments have the resources and capability of ending starvation and poverty immediately?

Is it not insanity to implement sanctions on some countries when their only effect is to punish the most vulnerable — as, for example, in Iraq, where because of U.S. and UN sanctions forty-five hundred Iraqi children die every month?

Is it not insanity that the developed countries — including Britain, currently the third largest exporter of arms in the world

— sell huge amounts of armaments to poor and developing countries, which in turn use much of the money allocated to them for aid to pay for these arms?

Is it not insanity that India's government — currently the third or fourth most powerful military machine in the world — continues to waste so many resources on militarism, while so many of its people are in need of the basic necessities of life?

Is it not insanity to continue destroying the environment by dumping radioactive materials and poisoning the oceans, polluting the air, and destroying the ozone?

Yes, it is insanity. I believe with Gandhi that the insanity of violence can only be stopped by the sanity of nonviolence. The time has come to renew our commitment, personally, politically, economically, and internationally, to the ancient wisdom of nonviolence.

As we move into the third millennium, we are beginning to realize that the human family is multi-ethnic, multicultural, and pluralistic in nature, and that if we are going to survive and develop, we need to learn to live together nonviolently.

In Rwanda, Bosnia, and to a lesser degree in Northern Ireland, we see the consequences of ethnic, political violence. We see how injustice and militarism breed fear and hatred and release murderous passions, drowning out all reason, compassion, and mercy. Many people prefer to believe that they are themselves too "civilized" to carry out such horrors, but we need honestly to face up to Gandhi's truth that each one of us, while capable of the greatest good, is also, given the right circumstances, capable of the greatest evil.

Creating a Culture of Nonviolence

In facing such problems we know that the "old" ways of violence, war, and militarism do not work. Fifty years after Gandhi's death, we are faced with a choice. Gandhi said, "There is no hope for the aching world except through the narrow and straight path of nonviolence." If we want to reap the harvest of peace and justice in the future, we will have to sow seeds of nonviolence. All of us need to take responsibility for the world's violence and, like Gandhi, pledge our lives to the nonviolent transformation of the world.

Gandhi taught that nonviolence does not mean passivity. It is the most daring, creative, and courageous way of living, and it is the only hope for the world. Nonviolence demands creativity. It pursues dialogue, seeks reconciliation, listens to the truth in our opponents, rejects militarism, and allows God's Spirit to transform us socially and politically.

But Gandhi's message of nonviolence is a challenge to the whole of humanity. Fifty years after his death, Gandhi challenges us to pursue a new millenium of nonviolence. This is not an impossible dream. In order to create a new culture of nonviolence, each of us can take several basic steps forward to help fulfill that dream.

First, we need to teach nonviolence to the children of the world — in India, Northern Ireland, and everywhere. Recently, twenty-two Nobel Peace Prize laureates asked the UN to declare the first decade of the new millennium as "a decade for a culture of nonviolence for the children of the world," in the hope that every nation will begin to educate its children in the way of nonviolence, in schools and homes. I was pleased during my visit to India to launch this movement, and to see the Gandhian movement giving an example to the world in the teaching of nonviolence in schools.

Second, as individuals, we can exercise the violence and untruth from our own lives. We can stop supporting systemic violence and militarism, and dedicate ourselves to nonviolent social change. We can take public stands for disarmament and justice, and take new risks for peace.

Third, we can urge the media to stop sensationalizing violence and instead highlight peaceful interactions, promote nonviolence, and uphold those who strive for real peace.

Fourth, we can embrace the wisdom of nonviolence that lies underneath each of the world's religions. Every religion contains the ancient truth of non-violence. Every religion needs to begin more and more to teach and promote nonviolence; and to worship the God of nonviolence. Gandhi said, "If religion does not teach us how to achieve the conquest of evil by overcoming it with goodness, it teaches us nothing." The world's religions need to come together in dialogue and respect, because there can be no world peace until the great religions make peace with one another. Perhaps the greatest contribution that those of us who come from a Christian tradition can make is to throw out the old just-war theory, embrace the nonviolence of Jesus, and refuse to kill one another, and truly follow his commandment to "love our enemies."

Fifth, we need to pursue Gandhi's dream of unarmed, international peacemaking teams, which resolve international conflict not through military solutions but nonviolent means. The world's governments need not only to reject military solutions, but also to create and finance international nonviolent conflict-resolution programs.

More than anything else, Gandhi inspires me by his great love for the poor. Perhaps the greatest contribution we can pay to Gandhi is to work to eliminate poverty from the face of the earth, Gandhi said that poverty is the worst form of violence. His memorial in India contains his parting advice, which we need to keep before us every day of our lives: "Recall the face of the poorest person you have ever seen, and ask yourself if the next step you take will be of any use to that person."

As we remember his death and celebrate his life, we dedicate ourselves to the wisdom of nonviolence. Shortly before his death, Gandhi said. "We are constantly being astonished these days at the amazing discoveries in the field of violence. But I maintain that far more undreamed of and seemingly impossible discoveries will be made in the field of nonviolence."

With Gandhi we can share great hope in a future filled with peace. Like Gandhi, we can make that hope a reality by pursuing new discoveries in the field of nonviolence, building a culture of non-violence for the new millenium, and becoming, like Gandhi, teachers and prophets of nonviolence.

As we exit the second millennium we can take great hope, too, from the many excellent achievements and discoveries made by millions of our brothers and sisters before us. They have, by their examples, enriched, inspired, and encouraged us to build lives of joy and peace for ourselves and for each other.

May the God of Mahatma Gandhi, the God of nonviolence, bless us all with peace, fill us with hope, and lead us and all humanity into a new world of nonviolence.

XVIII

Peace Prayers

Compiled by the Editors

Very early in life Mohandas K. Gandhi began to appreciate the universality of religion. He described them as highways leading to the same destination. As a mark of his respect for all religions and for all human beings he incorporated into his daily prayer relevant hymns from different faiths and he influenced millions in India to use them also. All these selected passages have the underlying theme of PEACE.

> My effort should never be to undermine another's faith but to make him a better follower of his own faith.
> – *M.K. Gandhi*

Gandhi Peace Prayers

Hindu Peace Prayer
I desire neither earthly kingdom, nor even freedom from birth and death. I desire only the deliverance from grief of all those afflicted by misery. Oh Lord, lead us from the unreal to the real; from darkness to light; from death to immortality. May there be peace in celestial regions. May there be peace on earth. May the waters be appeasing. May herbs be wholesome and may trees and plants bring peace to all. May all beneficent beings bring peace to us. May thy wisdom spread peace all through the world. May all things be a source of peace to all and to me. *Om Śānti, Śānti, Śānti* (Peace, Peace, Peace)

EDITORS

Islamic Peace Prayer
We think of Thee, worship Thee, bow to Thee as the Creator of this Universe; we seek refuge in Thee, the Truth, our only support. Thou art the Ruler, the barge in this ocean of endless births and deaths. In the name of Allah, the beneficent, the merciful. Praise be to the Lord of the Universe who has created us and made us into tribes and nations. Give us wisdom that we may know each other and not despise all things. We shall abide by thy Peace. And, we shall remember the servants of God are those who walk on this earth in humility and, when we address them, we shall say Peace Unto Us All.

Christian Peace Prayer
Blessed are the Peacemakers for they shall be known as The Children of God. But I say to you: Love your enemy, do good to those who hate you, bless those who curse you, pray for those who abuse you. To those who strike you on the cheek, offer the other also; and from those who take away your cloak, do not withhold your coat as well. Give to everyone who begs from you; and, to those who take away your goods, do not ask them again. And as you wish that others would do unto you, do so unto them as well.

Jewish Peace Prayer
Come let us go up to the mountain of the Lord, that we may walk the paths of the Most High. And we shall beat our swords into ploughshares and our spears into pruning hooks. Nation shall not lift up sword against nation - neither shall they learn war any more. And none shall be afraid, for the mouth of the Lord of Hosts has spoken.

Shinto Peace Prayer
Although the people living across the ocean surrounding us are all our brothers and sisters why, Oh Lord, is there trouble in this world? Why do winds and waves rise in the ocean surrounding us? I earnestly wish the wind will soon blow away all the clouds hanging over the tops of the mountains.

PEACE PRAYERS

Bahá'í Peace Prayer
Be generous in prosperity and thankful in adversity. Be fair in thy judgement and guarded in thy speech. Be a lamp unto those who walk in darkness and a home to the stranger. Be eyes to the blind and a guiding light unto the feet of the erring. Be a breath of life to the body of humankind, a dew to the soil of the human heart and a fruit upon the tree of humility.

More Peace Prayers

Vedic Prayers

May the earth be peaceful. May the atmosphere be peaceful. May the sky be peaceful. May the waters be peaceful. May the herbs be peaceful. May all the gods grant me peace. May each god grant me peace. May through peace every being attain peace. May through all these forms of peace I attain blessedness. Whatever is dreadful, whatever is cruel, and whatever is sinful in this world — may they all become peaceful. May everything confer blessedness upon us.
Atharva Veda 19:9.14

Meet together, speak together,
Let your minds be of one accord,
As the Gods of old, being of one mind,
Accepted their share of the sacrifice.

May your counsel be common, your assembly common,
Common the mind, and the thoughts of these united.
A common purpose do I lay before you,
And worship with your common oblation.

Let your aims be common,
And your hearts of one accord,
And all of you be of one mind,
So you may live well together.

Ṛg Veda 10:191.2-4

EDITORS

St. Francis of Assisi's Prayer for Peace
Lord, make me an instrument of your peace.
Where there is hatred, let me sow love
Where there is injury, pardon
Where there is doubt, faith
Where there is despair, hope
Where there is darkness, light
Where there is sadness, joy.

O Divine Master grant, that I may seek not so much
To be consoled as to console
To be understood as to understand
To be loved as to love;
For it is in giving that we receive;
It is in pardoning that we are pardoned;
It is in dying [to self] that we are born to eternal life.

A Gaelic Blessing
Deep peace of the running wave to you,
Deep peace of the flowing air to you,
Deep peace of the quiet earth to you,
Deep peace of the shining stars to you,
Deep peace of the gentle night to you,
Moon and stars pour their healing light on you.
Deep peace of Christ, the light of the world to you.

About the Authors

Abrams, Irwin

Irwin Abrams, distinguished University Professor Emeritus of Antioch University, is considered the leading authority on the history of the Nobel Peace Prize. He edited the authorized edition of the *Nobel Peace Lectures, 1971-1995*. He has been an advocate for peace his whole life. A Quaker, he participated in the wartime and postwar relief and reconstruction work of the American Friends Service Committee. He was the joint winner of the 1947 Nobel Peace Prize. Professor Abrams is currently revising his award-winning book, *The Nobel Peace Prize and Laureates*. He lives in Yellow Springs, Ohio.

Dear, John

John Dear is a Jesuit priest and the executive director of the Fellowship of Reconciliation, (FOR) the largest, oldest interfaith peace organization in the United States. He has worked among the homeless and needy in Washington, D.C., New York City, Richmond, Virginia, and El Salvador. He taught theology at Fordham University; and spent eight months in prison from 1993 to 1994 for a Plowshares antinuclear demonstration. His other books include *Peace behind Bars; Disarming the Heart; The God of Peace; The Sound of Listening, Jesus the Rebel; The Sacrament of Civil Disobedience*; and *Seeds of Nonviolence*. He has edited books by or about Henri Nouwen, Daniel Berrigan, and Nobel Laureate Mairead Corrigan Maguire. He lives in New York City.

ABOUT THE AUTHORS

Easwaran, Eknath

Eknath Easwaran was a writer and professor of English literature in India when he came to the U.S. as a Fulbright scholar. He founded the Blue Mountain Center of meditation in Berkeley. He taught meditation and allied skills to those who wanted to lead active and spiritually fulfilling lives. He wrote twenty-six books that are translated into eighteen languages. Sri Easwaran passed away on October 26, 1999.

Hallengren, Anders

Anders Hallengren is an associate professor of Comparative Literature and a research fellow in the Department of History of Literature and the History of Ideas at Stockholm University. He also serves as consulting editor for literature at Nobel e-Museum. Dr. Hallengren is a fellow of The Hemingway Society (USA) and was on the Steering Committee for the 1993 Guilin ELT/Hemingway International Conference in the People's Republic of China. Among his works in English are *The Code of Concord: Emerson's Search for Universal Laws; Gallery of Mirrors: Reflections of Swedenborgian Thought;* and *What is National Literature: Lectures on Emerson, Dostoevsky, Hemingway and the Meaning of Culture.*

Maguire, Mairead Corrigan

In 1977, Mairead Corrigan Maguire received the Nobel Peace Prize, along with Betty Williams, for their efforts for peace in Northern Ireland. The Peace People, as they called themselves, served as a catalyst to bring ordinary people into the struggle to end the violence and create a culture of peace in Northern Ireland. Maguire is a member of the international FOR and honorary president of the Appeal of the Nobel Peace Prize Laureates for a Decade of Nonviolence, which the United Nations endorsed

ABOUT THE AUTHORS

unanimously. She has traveled the world sharing the message of nonviolence. Her essay in this book was addressed to the Gandhian movement in India on the fiftieth anniversary of Gandhi's assassination

Rinpoche, Sogyal

Sogyal Rinpoche was born in Tibet and raised by one of the most revered spiritual masters of this century, Jamyang Khyentse Chökyi Lodrö. He travels and lectures throughout the world and is the founder and spiritual director of Rigpa, an international network of Buddhist groups and centers.

Roche, Douglas

Douglas Roche was elected to the Canadian Parliament four times, serving from 1972 to 1984 and specializing in the subjects of development and disarmament. He holds six honorary doctorates. Canada's ambassador for disarmament from 1984 to 1989, he was elected Chairman of the United Nation Disarmament Committee, the main UN body dealing with political and security issues, at the 43rd General Assembly in 1988. In 1995, he received the United Nations Association's Medal of Honour and the Papal Medal for his service on disarmament and security matters. In 2000, he received the Pomerance Award for work at the United Nations on nuclear disarmament. Roche is the author of sixteen books including *Bread Not Bombs: A Political Agenda for Social Justice*.

Roof, Jonathan

Jonathan Roof is a devotee of Shri Sathya Sai Baba.

ABOUT THE AUTHORS

Rush, Ann and John

Ann and John Rush are members of the Society of Friends in California, who did much to promote the work of Peace Pilgrim.

Swami Chinmayananda

Swami Chinmayananda, the founder of Chinmaya Mission, was a sage and visionary. He toured tirelessly all around the world giving discourses and writing commentaries on the scriptural knowledge of Vedanta, until he left his bodily form in 1993. (See write-up at the end of this book.)

Swami Pranavtirtha (1898 - 1974)

Paramahansa Parivrajak Swami Pranavtirtha was born of a Nagar brahmin family in Dwarka. He was named Rameshnath Ranganath before he initiated into *saṁnyāsa*. He was a dynamic orator, Secretary of Congress in Burma and was a contemporary and host to Mahatma Gandhi and Pandit Nehru. He became a disciple of Swami Swayamjyotitirtha and the fourth dynasty of Swami Ramatirtha. He is the author of some 42 books in English and Gujarati including *Living the Gita*, *Says Yagnavalkya*, *Immortality*, and *Gujarati-English Vedantic Dictionary*. He lived in Abu for many years before he moved to Zambia in 1967 until his *Mahasamadhi* in 1974.

Swami Tejomayananda

Swami Tejomayananda, the spiritual head of Chinmaya Mission centers worldwide since 1993, is fulfilling the vision of his guru, Swami Chinmayananda. As Mission head, Swami Tejomayananda has already conducted more than 400 *jñāna yajña* worldwide. He has served as dean or *Ācārya* of the

ABOUT THE AUTHORS

Sandeepany Institutes of Vedanta, both in India and in California. Fluent in Hindi, Marathi and English, and lecturing and writing commentaries in all three languages he makes even the most complicated Vedantic topics clear to his audience.

H.H. Jagadguru Shankaracharya Shri Bharati Tirtha Mahaswamigal

Shri Sringeri Sharada Peetha has had a continuing line of succession of *Ācārya*. The *Ācārya* have all been men of great erudition, spiritual attainment and compassion. Known as the Jagadguru, each one of them has added to the lustre of the *Pīṭha* [Monastry].

The present *Ācārya*, His Holiness Jagadguru Shri Bharati Tirtha Mahaswamigal, is 36th in the line of succession of Sringeri lineage. He is always engaged in the welfare of his disciples and devotees. His knowledge of the scriptures is unparalleled. His learning is vast and spiritual attainment immense.

He was initiated into *saṁnyāsa* in 1974 by His Holiness Shri Abhinava Vidyatirtha, under whom he mastered the *śāstra* [scriptures] in just eight years.

Vaswani, J.P.

Dada Jashan P. Vaswani is the spiritual head of Sadhu Vaswani Mission in Pune, India. He was born on August 2, 1918, at Hyderabad-Sind, in a pious Sindhi family. He is credited to have started the first all girl's college, St. Mira's College, which now has an enrollment of 5000 students. He is the author of about 30 books in English and several more in Sindhi.

Vrajaprana, Pravrajika

Pravrajika Vrajaprana is a nun of the Vedanta Society of Southern California at Sarada Convent, Santa Barbara, USA.